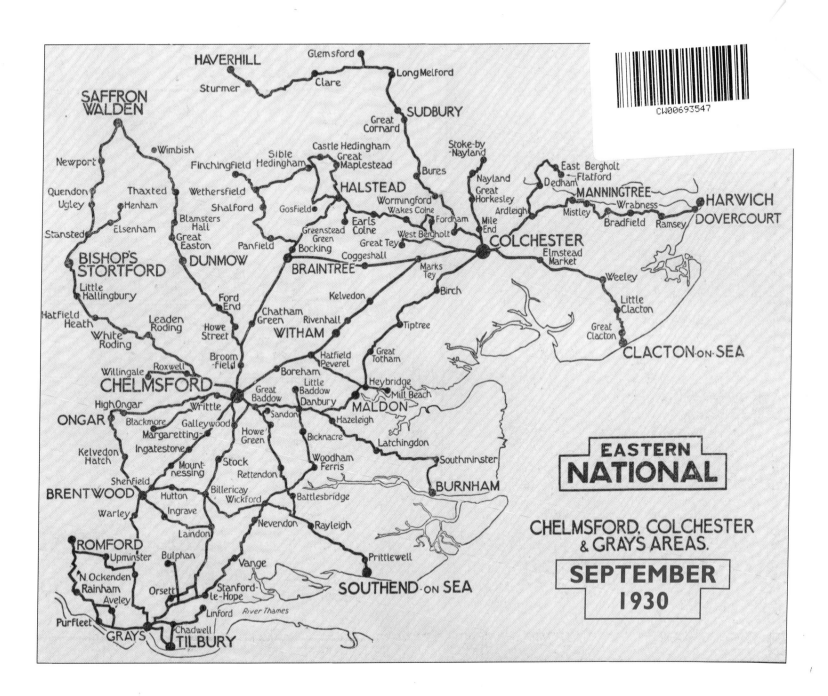

EASTERN
NATIONAL

CHELMSFORD, COLCHESTER
& GRAYS AREAS.

SEPTEMBER
1930

Eastern National

Richard Delahoy

Contents

First published 2003

ISBN 0 7110 2952 0

Published by Ian Allan Publishing

an imprint of Ian Allan Publishing Ltd, Hersham, Surrey KT12 4RG.

Printed by Ian Allan Printing Ltd, Hersham, Surrey KT12 4RG.

Code: 0309/B

Introduction

Picture the scene: a classic, almost timeless Eastern Coach Works body on a solid, dependable Bristol chassis, resplendent in dignified Tilling green and cream, gold underlined fleetname, smartly turned-out crew (of two, of course!), carrying a wide social mix of passengers who depend on the bus for shopping, work and pleasure trips. These were the 'glory days' of Eastern National as many will remember it. Of course, it wasn't always thus. The Tilling influence didn't really make itself felt until the mid-1930s (Tilling having bought a controlling interest in 1931), and World War 2 hardly merits the 'glory' epithet, even if the company did perform a Herculean task in incredibly trying circumstances. For many, the glory days were probably the 1950s and early 1960s — interestingly, the period when the fleet achieved a very high degree of standardisation and hence *could* have been accused of being boring. But there was a richness that made the company and its operations interesting. I hope to convey some of that richness through this book.

I was born in 1955, so, by the time that I was old and observant enough to appreciate what the bus industry had to offer, the glory days were arguably in decline, as increasing costs, staff shortages, traffic congestion and permanent shifts in social and demographic trends conspired to strangle companies like Eastern National. As I write I have in front of me a 1965 leaflet cataloguing a long list

Timeless classic No 1: solid and dependable, the Bristol K type was the mainstay of the fleet for many years, albeit with the inconvenient sunken-gangway lowbridge ECW body. No 4114 (RPU 524) was one of seven KS models delivered in 1950. Displaying its 1954 number (1349), it rounds Southend's Victoria Circus. Note the hand signal — no trafficators in those days! Renumbered again in 1964 as 2306, it lasted until 1967.
Richard Delahoy collection

of journeys that were being 'temporarily withdrawn due to the staff shortage becoming more acute'. The anonymous writer expressed the hope that 'by announcing these pre-determined cuts the company will be able to maintain other journeys on a more reliable basis'. History tells us that the standards of reliability achieved in the glory days have proved hard, if not impossible, to replicate since. But let's not become too maudlin and instead celebrate those days.

Inevitably, defining the 'glorious' era is somewhat subjective. A convenient and sensible starting point is 1930, when the company registered the previous year actually began trading, as successor to the National Omnibus & Transport Co. Defining the end point for this study is more difficult, but a number of events point to 1969: the first rear-engined buses — both single- and double-deck, in the form of Bristol RELLs and VRs — were delivered, representing a new era in bus design, at least so far as Eastern National was concerned. (Rear-engined *coaches* — also Bristol REs — had, of course, joined the fleet somewhat earlier, in 1964, but were more evolutionary than revolutionary in terms of their impact on the company's operations.) January 1969 also saw the company's ownership move from the Transport Holding Co — state-owned but still very much following the principles of the former Tilling Group — to the new National Bus Company (NBC), and we all know where that was to

Timeless classic No 2: solid and dependable, yes, but Bristol L5G/ECW ONO 42 and her sisters dated quickly once underfloor-engined saloons were introduced. Delivered in 1949 as 4021, she is seen in later life as 303, laying over in Brentwood. The ECW body seated 35, thus not taxing the Gardner 5LW engine too much.
Richard Delahoy collection

lead. National leaf-green livery (unrelieved, in many cases) and double-N fleetnames have no place in this particular celebration of Eastern National, but that is not to decry the later history of the company and the achievements of the NBC era or the subsequent privatisation.

It is often overlooked that until 1952 Eastern National operated through two entirely separate areas — the Midland section, with headquarters in Bedford, and the Eastern section, based at the overall Head Office in Chelmsford. Under the British Transport Commission the Midland section was transferred to United Counties in 1952, Eastern National gaining control of Westcliff-on-Sea Motor Services (which by then incorporated the City Coach Co and the twin Benfleet/Canvey businesses) by way of compensation. The history of the Midland section is really better understood within the context of the story of United Counties, but one chapter is devoted to what really ought to have been 'Midland National'. In dealing with new vehicles acquired up to 1952 I have, however, included all deliveries, whether for the Eastern or Midland areas, since it is impossible to do otherwise.

Growing up in Westcliff-on-Sea, I regarded Eastern National buses as a part of the daily routine, taken for granted, even if my schools were so close to home that I didn't need to catch a bus. Shopping in Southend was easy, the 6/6A routes with LD-style Lodekkas providing a 15-minute headway. Opposite the 6A stop

an OMO saloon — MW or LS — would take us to Leigh-on-Sea and the delights of the cockle-sheds, while the still-KSW-operated 17 was only a couple of streets away and led to the beach at Chalkwell. My greatest delight, however, was to walk down to the main A127, with its FLF Lodekkas on the former City Coach Co 251 service from Southend to distant Wood Green in North London, as well as on more local services such as the 22/A/B.

Many people have helped in bringing together the material for this celebration of Eastern National. Thanks go, in no particular order, to Alan Osborne, Martin Weyell, Peter Snell, Frank Church, John Boylett, Paul Harrison, Chris Stewart, Lyn Watson, Philip Wallis, Arnold Richardson, Kevin Lane, Michael Dryhurst, Alan Cross, John Taylor and John Wilson. I am also greatly indebted to all the photographers who agreed to allow their pictures to be used, and apologise to any who could not be traced. For the text I have drawn heavily on three invaluable sources: *The Years Between, 1909-1969*, Crawley, MacGregor and Simpson's definitive history of the National Omnibus & Transport Co and its successors; the PSV Circle's *Eastern National Fleet History*; and, finally, the publications and news-sheets of the Eastern National Enthusiasts' Group (now the Essex Bus Enthusiasts' Group — www.essexbus.org.uk).

Now, sit back and prepare to be transported to the glory days of the Eastern National Omnibus Co. Enjoy the ride!

Richard Delahoy MCIT
Southend-on-Sea, March 2003

Prologue

The Eastern National Omnibus Company Ltd — often abbreviated to ENOC — was registered at Companies House on 28 February 1929, but to understand the history we need to go back to Thomas Clarkson's National Steam Car Co Ltd of 1909. Clarkson was an engineer and inventor and had developed various steam-propelled road vehicles, culminating in an eight-seat Brougham named the 'Chelmsford' — he had established a factory there in 1902 — which he exhibited at the 1903 Automobile Show at Crystal Palace. Further development led to an order for eight 14-seat buses for the newly formed Torquay & District Motor Omnibus Co. More orders soon followed from around the country, and double-deckers were supplied to the London General Omnibus Co in 1905, but Clarkson found it difficult to break into the London market. In 1908 he demonstrated the potential of his steam double-deckers by transporting the Territorial Army from Chelmsford to Latchingdon in four buses (carrying up to 50 people each), assisted by a steam car and van. By the time of a second run for the Essex Yeomanry in May 1909 the buses carried the fleetname 'NATIONAL', establishing a precedent that was to last — just — into 2003, when the corporate 'First' style finally supplanted 'Eastern National'.

Unable to achieve meaningful sales in London, Clarkson was introduced to a firm of bankers, which helped him set up the National Steam Car Co to begin bus operations in central London in his own right on 2 November 1909. From just four buses, the fleet grew rapidly to around 180 by 1913, carrying over 24 million passengers a year. Unsurprisingly, the dominant London General Omnibus Co (LGOC) viewed his expansion with alarm and in 1913 reached an agreement with National which in effect made the latter an LGOC franchisee from 1 January 1914, albeit trading under the National name.

Meanwhile, and much more relevant to our story, National had started running buses in its 'home' town of Chelmsford in July 1913 by acquiring the services run by the Great Eastern Railway. The GER's pioneering 1905 petrol-engined buses were

not acquired but were replaced by Clarkson steamers, and the services expanded. Operations also started at Colchester in 1914 but had to be withdrawn as a result of World War 1 and were not resumed until 1919.

The appointment in 1918 of Walter Iden as joint Managing Director of National heralded a move away from steam propulsion. Iden had been Chief Engineer of the LGOC and Manager of its bus-building arm, AEC, and he lost no time in replacing the steamers with AECs. In 1919 National withdrew from London but took over a defunct General garage in Bedford, the LGOC being precluded from running there itself by the terms of a territorial agreement signed with the BET group. Thus was born the Midland area, to be discussed further in Chapter 6.

With the existing base at Chelmsford, and Colchester operations re-established after World War 1, the 1920s saw rapid expansion across much of Essex. Clarkson continued unsuccessfully to try to develop commercially viable steam vehicles until he resigned in 1921, a year after the company had been renamed to the more appropriate National Omnibus & Transport Co Ltd. Through the opening up of new routes, National's presence in Essex grew rapidly in the unrestrained

Clarkson began steam-bus operations in Essex just before World War 1. This is ostensibly a shot of two National steamers at Market Hill, Coggeshall, but the bus on the right (F 8536) was in fact operated by Moore Bros of Kelvedon, which firm would not be acquired by Eastern National until 1963. Taken on 8 April 1914, the photograph was posed by Clarkson to obtain publicity for his buses. The bus on the left was a genuine National, but the company did not operate to Coggeshall until somewhat later. *Eastern National collection, c/o Essex Bus Enthusiasts' Group*

National progressed from steam buses to AECs like 2152 (LH 8480), a B type acquired from the LGOC in 1921, with a Hurst Nelson 34-seat body. It operated from a new yard at the Anchor Inn in Bishops Stortford on route 13 to Saffron Walden, a service that still exists today as the 301, now run under contract to Essex County Council by Stansted Transit. *Eastern National collection, c/o Essex Bus Enthusiasts' Group*

Dual-door layouts were in vogue when 2383 (TM 8936) was delivered in 1927, being one of a small number of Associated Daimlers to join the National fleet. It is seen working between Hitchin and Biggleswade but passed to United Counties in 1933 as part of the transfer of the depot and some routes at Stony Stratford. *L. F. Watson collection*

No 2925 (VX 1560), a Gilford CP6 with Strachans body, no doubt proved a nippy opponent for the many small operators in Grays but could not have been very economic, with only 20 seats yet requiring a crew of two. Built in 1929, it passed to London Transport in 1933, as explained in Chapter 5. *J. F. Higham collection, courtesy L. F. Watson*

No 3028 (TM 6306) was a 1930 AEC Regent with 50-seat Shorts lowbridge body, registered in Bedford. By the time Michael Dryhurst found it in Chelmsford bus station it had migrated eastwards and had been rebuilt by Beadle during the war. Renumbered 1143 in 1954, it was withdrawn after 26 years' service — not a bad record!
Michael Dryhurst

years before the 1930 Road Traffic Act brought in the system of quality and quantity licensing that was to last for over 50 years. Elsewhere, from modest beginnings in Stroud in 1919, the company also came to dominate much of southwest England, both by opening up new territory and by some major acquisitions.

National's involvement in London was resurrected in 1921. Based on a similar structure proposed by the East Surrey Traction Co, National and the LGOC reached an agreement for what was defined as the 'London Country Area', an area beyond the Metropolitan Police district and extending to include Romford, Brentwood, Epping, Bishops Stortford, Hertford, Hitchin, Luton, Watford, St Albans, Hemel Hempstead and Rickmansworth. Within this area the LGOC would provide the buses and premises, with National running them effectively as an agent and risk-sharing partner — an arrangement that continued until operations were transferred to the newly formed London General Country Services in 1932. A fascinating and complex story (and one that would elicit very

close interest from the competition authorities, were it repeated today!), it falls outside the remit of this book.

By 1928, when the 'big four' railway companies formed by the 1923 Grouping had acquired powers to operate bus services, National was operating in all four territories. It was agreed that the bus operations be split into four geographic companies, based on the railway boundaries, with National itself becoming a holding company, as a prelude to the railway companies each taking a 50% share in one of the operating companies. Thus in 1929 were formed Western National, Southern National, Eastern National and Midland National, along with a fifth, non-trading company, Northern National, registered to protect rights to the name. However, as the LMS and LNER railway boundaries were so intertwined, Midland never traded, and the operations in that area became the Midland area of ENOC itself, with the LMS and LNER each taking a 25% ownership of ENOC.

The stage was set for our story to start.

National allocated body numbers as well as fleetnumbers to identify vehicles in its fleet. This plate was recovered from 2788, an all-Leyland TD1 of 1928, whose body was found in a field in Clacton in 1976 alongside that of 2902, a contemporary AEC Regent.

7

1. The Early 1930s — Consolidation

In 1932 ENOC bought a quartet of these massive beasts — AEC Renowns with 66-seat Short bodies, all registered by the Midland Section. Probably still with its original AEC petrol engine, No 3332 (MJ 406) awaits the crowds for Whipsnade Zoo; in 1936 it received a Gardner 5LW oil (diesel) unit. It was scrapped in 1949. *J. F. Higham collection, courtesy L. F. Watson*

The transition from National to Eastern National was not initially apparent to the public, but behind the scenes there were major changes in the ownership. The new ENOC was capitalised at £500,000 and duly purchased the National assets corresponding to the Midland and Eastern areas for £400,000. Only the London coaching division and the Grays area operations were excluded at first, as explained later.

The Eastern National name appeared on timetables from May 1930. The fleet was formally transferred in June, comprising a mixed bag of about 275 buses. At one ▲ extreme were 82 by now ancient-looking AEC Y types which had been rebodied between 1926 and 1928, the majority being open-top double-deckers. Dating from 1927-9 but already superseded in design terms by the lower-built Leyland Tiger was a substantial fleet of 77 Leyland Lions, most with 32-seat rear-entrance bus bodywork. The most recent saloons were 15 examples of Leyland's TS-series Tiger, whose classic design set the standard until underfloor-engined buses became commonplace in the 1950s.

Leyland had also been the favoured choice for double-deckers since 1928, when 22 TD1 Titans introduced the lowbridge, side-gangway layout; the first 13 retained an open staircase, but later deliveries were enclosed. Dual sourcing was evident in 1929 and 1930, with 13 AEC Regents and a quintet of Reliance saloons. Finally there was an eclectic mix of non-standard vehicles, ranging from Ford, Chevrolet, GMC and Burford minibuses (not that the term had been coined then), sundry Dennises and Daimlers and a quartet of nippy Gilford CP6s through to a massive three-axle Guy FCX double-decker. Fleetnumbers were spread over the old National range, from 2001 (a Dodson-bodied AEC YC of 1919) to 3030 (a Short-bodied AEC Regent that was to last until 1956). Subsequent deliveries continued the 3000 series through to 4233, until the fleet was renumbered in 1954.

As early as September 1930, short routes started to be linked to offer lengthy cross-country facilities, with some buses running from Harwich right through to Tilbury Ferry. By the end of the year, ENOC was running 55 routes in the Eastern Section and a further 88 in the Midland (see maps inside the covers), including a number started during the year in the frantic rush to stake out its territory ahead of the new licensing system about to be introduced by the 1930 Road Traffic Act. The Act was to have a profound effect in setting common, national standards in place of the *ad hoc* and sometimes decidedly partial 'regulation' by local Watch Committees. Fundamental to the Act was the protection offered to licensed services, effectively preventing competition. This was to lead to many small and medium-sized operators' selling out to ENOC, which gradually acquired a near-monopoly in many parts of its operating area.

The Act also created much greater financial stability, encouraging investment in new buses and facilities. For ENOC and the other members of the National group, that stability was to have far-reaching implications when it tempted Thomas Tilling Ltd to buy a controlling interest in February 1931. Like the National, Tilling had started out as London bus operator and similarly built up a substantial presence there, but by agreement with the General was restricted to 150 buses in the capital. It also ran in Brighton and, through a joint venture with the BET group (Tilling & British Automobile Traction Ltd), had interests in a number of other major companies. The Tilling Group was one of the defining forces in the bus industry, and its influence shaped almost all of ENOC's glory days.

In the early part of the decade, ENOC moved quickly to consolidate its position by acquiring the 69 vehicles and 28 routes of the combined Silver Queen/ Enterprise businesses in Clacton. This was to be ENOC's largest single acquisition of the 1930s and 1940s. Silver Queen had been established in 1913 as Clacton & District Motor Services Ltd, but operations were almost completely suspended during World War 1. From 1919, however, there was rapid expansion, so that by 1922 its network was almost complete; in 1926 it adopted the Silver Queen name.

Interestingly, it also had substantial operations around Grantham, Lincoln, Louth and Retford; Lincolnshire Road Car Co was set up in 1928 to acquire that part of the business. In 1922 competition started from A. Fitch & Sons, later renamed the Enterprise Bus Co, but by the latter part of the decade a degree of co-ordination had been agreed, with Silver Queen buying Enterprise in 1930 before selling out to ENOC the following year. The takeover plugged an important gap in ENOC's territory, giving the company control of the Tendring Hundred, taking in Walton-on-the-Naze, Harwich and Dovercourt as well as Clacton itself. The acquired vehicles presented an interesting mix, ranging from modern Leyland Titans and Tigers to 17 Thornycroft J types — mostly with LGOC K-type double-deck bodies — and 20 small Chevrolets. Enterprise's contribution included single examples of the new AEC Regal and Regent and far more exotic single-deckers from Lancia, Gotfriedson and Berliet.

New purchases by ENOC in 1931 were more predictable — well, almost! Dual sourcing saw Leyland and AEC share both the single- and double-deck orders, but more unusual were an experimental quintet of Thornycroft XC 'deckers — a type not bought new before or subsequently. They proved underpowered and were later re-engined, and later still all but one received new ECW bodies. Even odder were a pair of PLSC3 Lions, a type no

longer in production; the chassis dated from 1927/8 and had been stored by National. Strachans was favoured with all the body orders, except for a pair of Duple coaches on Tiger TS1 chassis.

The year 1932 was to provide further variety, with the introduction of Tilling Stevens B39A7s and Dennis Lancets, all with Beadle single-deck bus bodies, alongside more Titans, Tigers, Regents and Regals. AEC's contribution included a quartet of three-axle Renowns, but AEC was never to supply another new bus to ENOC after 1932, apparently after it was discovered that the Southall manufacturer was supplying the company's rivals at lower prices! AEC did introduce one lasting legacy into the fleet in 1931, as AEC Regent 3063 was fitted with an early oil (diesel) engine. It was not, however, until the middle of the decade that diesel engines, with their much better fuel economy, became standard.

Many buses of this era would be heavily modified and rebuilt or rebodied in the following decade, to extend their lives at a time when new buses were almost unobtainable. From 1936 onwards many also acquired Gardner diesel engines, replacing the original, smooth but thirsty petrol units. Leyland Tiger 3304 (MJ 401) is a good example: new as a petrol-engined 26-seat coach, by the time it was withdrawn 19 years later, in 1951, it had metamorphosed into a 32-seat bus with a Gardner 5LW engine and Bristol radiator.

The open frontage of Chelmsford's 1929 bus station was shortly to be swept away when this shot was taken *c*1935. Four of the five Thornycroft XCs dominate the line-up, joined by an AEC Regent and a Leyland Titan.
Eastern National collection, c/o Essex Bus Enthusiasts' Group

In 1931 ENOC made its biggest acquisition of the decade — Clacton-based Silver Queen. Delivered the year before, all-Leyland TD1 VX 5304 became ENOC 3169, as seen here on the 107, formerly a joint Silver Queen/Enterprise service.
W. J. Haynes / Richard Delahoy collection

2. The Mid- and Late 1930s —
Towards a Monopoly

The Borough Motor Services was acquired in 1933 but maintained as a separate subsidiary until 1940. No 3441 (MY 2542), an ex-demonstration AEC Regent of 1929 with typical 'piano-front' Shorts body, thus displays Borough names but an ENOC cast fleetnumber plate. Its destination is somewhat overshadowed by advertising. Perhaps surprisingly, the bus lasted only until 1938. *Alan B. Cross*

The years from 1933 saw ENOC make over 40 separate acquisitions as it sought to dominate its territory, both in Essex and in Bedfordshire. This was tempered by the loss of part of the Grays operations and other effects of the formation of the London Passenger Transport Board in 1933, as will be discussed in Chapter 5.

One area where National and ENOC were seriously under-represented was the southeastern corner of Essex, taking in Southend, Rayleigh, Hadleigh and Benfleet. Southend Corporation Transport had introduced trams in 1901, and trolleybuses followed in 1925; an initial experience with motor buses in 1914-16 had not been successful, but limited bus operations recommenced in 1932. Meanwhile, Westcliff-on-Sea Motor Services Ltd had developed into a substantial business, running not only local services but also long trunk routes to Grays and Romford. A number of other independents served the

local area, whilst ENOC viewed with alarm the growth of Rayleigh Motor Services, which in July 1930 started a Southend–Maldon–Colchester route. Another contender was The Borough Services Ltd, like Westcliff operating services in Southend and Leigh and also running to Grays.

Unable to expand further after the passing of the 1930 Act, the directors of The Borough Services instead acquired an interest in Rayleigh Motor Services and thus became a more serious threat to ENOC, and it came as no surprise when ENOC bought out Borough in May 1933. The Colchester service had been sold to Borough in 1932, and in June 1933 Westcliff obtained a controlling interest in the Rayleigh business, which was operated as a separate subsidiary until its licences and buses were transferred to Westcliff in 1936. Meanwhile, in 1935, Westcliff itself came under Tilling control but was maintained entirely separately from ENOC until the 1950s. Because of existing territorial agreements, ENOC continued to run Borough as a subsidiary company until 1940. Eighteen Borough vehicles joined the ENOC fleet, although technically they were licensed to Borough and for some while carried 'Borough' names on Eastern National livery. The fleet mainly comprised AEC Regent double-deckers and Gilford saloons, various ENOC vehicles being drafted into the Borough fleet as these were withdrawn.

Elsewhere in Essex, consolidation continued. Some of the more significant businesses acquired included Bird Motor Services, Horn Coach Co, Johnson of Colne Engaine, Griffiths' Pullman service, East Bergholt & District, Underwoods of East Mersea, Berry of Colchester, Quest Motors of Maldon, Patten of Wickford and Clavering & District. Some of these brought with them express services into London, from Maldon and Braintree.

A far less satisfactory takeover was of part of Edward Hillman's services from Bow, in east London. His modern, comfortable and fast Gilford coaches beat hands down the competition from the LGOC and ENOC, so that by 1933 he was running over 90 vehicles, with 51 scheduled journeys a day from Bow to Chelmsford, some extended on to Colchester and into East Anglia. His operations cut right across the London Transport boundary — a situation that could not continue under the new

legislation — so Hillman compelled LT to take over his Upminster and Brentwood services, and LT eventually bought his entire business. In so doing LT came to an arrangement that ENOC would acquire the Clacton and East Anglian services as well as the Bow–Chelmsford workings. ENOC then came to an agreement with Grey-Green and Eastern Counties to surrender (for a fee) the East Anglian licences but also lost out, as its application to run to Clacton was refused. The company had intended to halve (to hourly) the frequency of the Bow service, because of the ban on carrying local traffic within London, but in the event continued the old Hillman frequency. The service, latterly numbered 30, lasted until 1968, when it was diverted to Wood Green as the 351.

No 3160 (VW 6216), a 1928 Leyland Tiger TS2 acquired from Silver Queen, was rebodied by Eastern Counties in 1935 as seen here, complete with roll-back roof, but was withdrawn only five years later. *Eastern National collection, c/o Essex Bus Enthusiasts' Group*

All the acquisitions brought into the fleet a rich variety, too varied to list here, although it is questionable whether the engineering department appreciated that richness, as, under Tilling influence, a high degree of standardisation was starting to emerge in the choice of new vehicle purchases. Bodywork from Eastern Counties (later to be Eastern Coach Works) appeared for the first time in 1933, beginning an association that was to last until ECW built its final bodies in 1986. Tilling initially favoured Dennis, so 30 Lancets formed the bulk of 1933's intake, with just a solitary Leyland Tiger coach and seven Titans, one with a Park Royal body. A similar pattern was followed in 1934, with a very modest influx of only 22 new vehicles — 20 Lancets and a pair of Titans, all Eastern Counties-bodied. Deliveries picked up again in 1935, with 46 new vehicles joining the fleet. Twenty-four were the almost inevitable Dennis Lancets with Eastern Counties bus bodies, but these were joined by 14 'flying pigs' — Dennis Aces with 20-seat Dennis bodywork, some of which were one-man-operated. A pair of Lancet coaches and six more Titans completed the roll-call.

By 1936 the Dennis era was drawing to a close. The year's deliveries included six forward-control Ace coaches, but Bristol was about to reign supreme. Eastern Counties' body works, to become ECW in 1937, was already owned by Tilling, and the group had taken full control of the Bristol Tramways & Carriage Co, including its manufacturing business, in 1935. Henceforth it was inevitable that Bristol and ECW products would start to dominate Tilling fleets, aided by Bristol's legendary reliability and economy, especially when married to the equally legendary Gardner 5LW diesel engine. (Indeed, there are still a few Bristol/ECW buses in the successor fleet in 2003.) Interestingly, the single-deck element — 19 JO5G models — all had dual-

purpose seating and forward entrances; the 13 GO5G 'deckers were more conventional, with lowbridge 53-seat Brush bodies. The remainder of the 1936 intake comprised six Leyland TD4s, also Brush-bodied.

It was not only in new vehicles that ENOC was making a substantial investment. Impressive new bus stations were built at Clacton, Maldon and Bedford, with new or rebuilt garages at Dovercourt, Walton-on-the-Naze, Halstead, Hitchin, Huntingdon and Aylesbury. In Chelmsford the combined bus station and garage, which had only been opened in 1929, was partly demolished and replaced by one three times larger, covering 57,000sq ft and offering 550ft of departure stands, overseen by a control room. (It has survived into 2003, still in use but looking well past its best; it is due to be replaced shortly.) The new buildings conformed to a modern, distinctive Tilling house style by architect H. J. Starkey that bore more than a passing resemblance to Charles Holden's far better-known (and better-preserved) designs for London Transport.

By the end of the decade, Eastern National's management could be justifiably proud of their achievements. The Road Traffic Act had brought order out of the chaos of the 1920s and enabled companies like ENOC to achieve dominant positions. The railway shareholdings had permitted a modest degree of co-operation, such as through or inter-available tickets, and the financial strength of the Tilling Group had enabled the company to buy up much of the opposition. But ENOC did not have a monopoly. Its Tilling cousin, Westcliff-on-Sea Motor Services, dominated much of the southeast corner of Essex, with Southend Corporation, the Benfleet and Canvey companies and the City Coach Co all significant players there. Elsewhere there were substantial independents such as Hicks of Braintree and Moores of Kelvedon, plus Colchester Corporation. A similar situation existed in the Midland area, where Luton Corporation had at least one thing in common with Colchester — both had rebuffed takeover approaches from ENOC. Southend had likewise rejected overtures by Tilling, on behalf of Westcliff.

Before considering the impact of World War 2, let us look at the new vehicle deliveries for 1937 and 1938. The move to Bristol/ECW products was swift. The 1937 intake of 73 buses and coaches included 53 Bristols — JO saloons and GO and K 'deckers; Leyland provided 18 Tigers and Titans and Dennis a pair of Lancets. By the following year Leyland was out of favour, not to reappear until nine years later; the 51 new buses (no coaches this year) were all Bristol K5Gs or L5Gs, save for a trio of Lancets — Dennis's last vehicles for the fleet until the Dart burst onto the scene in the 1990s.

As well as the inevitable mixed bag of buses that came with acquired businesses, 10 Tilling-Stevens of 1929/30 vintage were bought second-hand from the North Western Road Car Co in 1938; these lasted only until 1940-2. A more enduring legacy came with the 1938 purchase from Hants & Dorset of a pair of Leyland TD1s with open-top Short bodywork, for use on a seasonal service at Clacton. Dedicated open-top seaside bus services were later to become an important aspect of ENOC's operations at Clacton and Southend.

The final years of peace also witnessed a substantial programme of rebodying, 26 of the 1928/9 Leyland Lions receiving new bodywork by Beadle or ECW in 1938 and a further six being similarly treated in 1939. With the benefit of hindsight, it was unfortunate that no completely new vehicles were delivered in 1939, for new buses would be scarce for the next six years!

◄ With its distinctive snout, it was no wonder the Dennis Ace earned the epithet 'flying pig'! Freshly out of the Dennis factory — which built the body as well as the chassis — is 3596 (CTW 192). New in 1935, it had a respectable (15-year) career. *Eastern National collection, c/o Essex Bus Enthusiasts' Group*

★ ★ ★ ★ ★ ★ ★ ★

BRIEF DETAILS *of the*

EASTERN NATIONAL

NEW LUXURY : COACHES :
for the
1937 - SEASON

MORE AND STILL BETTER COACHES
for Your Comfort !

★ ★ ★ ★ ★ ★ ★ ★ ★ ★ ★ ★ ★ ★ ★ ★ ★ ★ ★

In 1936 Dennis was largely supplanted by Bristol as the favoured supplier of single-deck chassis. Representing the new order is 240 (DEV 460), seen outside West Mersea garage in 1955. Originally numbered 3624, it carries an ECW body fitted in 1943 and would last a further four years before passing to a London dealer. *Frank Church*

In 1936/7 Bristol replaced Leyland as supplier of double-deck chassis. Initial deliveries of GO models were followed by K types in 1938, 3812 (GTW 893) being one of 20 new that year. In later years, carrying its 1954 number (1266), it waits on the forecourt of Southend Victoria station, terminus for many years of ENOC's long-distance services, before Southend garage was adapted as a bus station. *R. F. Mack*

The author makes no apologies for including this superb official photograph, showing comparatively rare Eastern Counties-bodied Dennis Lancet 3686 (ENO 964), one of a pair new in 1937. Note the roof-mounted luggage carrier, fittings for a side destination board and curtained windows. No doubt the more luxurious features were lost when it was rebuilt twice by Beadle during the war. After withdrawal in 1953 it passed to a haulage contractor.
Eastern Coach Works official photograph, courtesy M. Doggett

14

3. Wartime Trials and Triumphs

At the outbreak of war in September 1939 one of the first tasks successfully completed by ENOC was the evacuation of around 40,000 mothers and children away from vulnerable towns and cities. ENOC's role was usually to take the evacuees to a suitable railhead for their onward journey to hopefully safer areas. The first service changes came with the announcement of wartime winter schedules from 23 September, involving the withdrawal of some seasonal routes and selective cuts elsewhere, particularly in the evenings.

The blackout — designed to protect against enemy bomber aircraft — was largely responsible for the evening reductions. Driving with just a single, hooded headlamp was difficult and dangerous, and conductors and passengers had little or no light inside; later, white markings were introduced on mudguards and rear corners to make them a little easier to see. An interesting consequence of wartime shortages was the introduction in 1943

of fixed bus stops, designed to reduce the tyre rubber and fuel that was wasted with frequent unplanned stops. Contemporary publicity warned: 'This means that your 'Bus may no longer be able to pick you up or set you down just where it has done for years, but please be tolerant and help the Conductors who are doing their best to assist you.'

The war presented some opportunities for consolidation. As recounted earlier, the Borough services and vehicles were transferred to ENOC in October 1940 (although the company itself was not wound up until 1947), while the services of Simpson's of Leaden Roding were bought in 1940, along with two buses. The impact on passenger traffic varied across the company's territory. For instance, some seaside towns, such as Clacton and Southend, saw dramatic declines in population, due to the threat of invasion and the designation of 'restricted areas'. Others, like Chelmsford, saw major increases in peak traffic to

In this view of Chelmsford bus station, taken from the adjacent railway viaduct, white-painted rear corners are prominent on all the buses, Bristol K5G 3812 (GTW 893) being nearer the camera. The garage later suffered a direct hit from German bombs in May 1943, destroying 25 buses.
Charles F. Klapper collection, courtesy The Omnibus Society

serve factories, such as Marconi,
Hoffman and Crompton Parkinson,
busily engaged on war work.
Increased capacity was created by
converting many single-deckers to
inward-facing, perimeter seating,
allowing more standing room —
uncomfortable but very necessary!
To cover for men called up to serve in
the Forces, women were employed
in a variety of roles, including as
conductresses, but driving remained
a largely male preserve.

Longer-distance services were
some of those most affected by the
need to conserve scarce resources.
The summer coastal express routes did
not run at all during the war, and all-
year-round routes from London, like
the B to Halstead and the C to Maldon,
were reduced and then withdrawn
altogether. The former Hillman's route to Bow was also truncated
at Brentwood from 1942 to 1946.

With no indigenous supplies of oil or petrol, conserving fuel
became a high priority. The mid-1930s move to diesel (oil)
engines had helped, as they often achieved twice the miles per
gallon of the petrol-engined fleet. That was not enough, however,
and ENOC's Chief Engineer William Morison was at the
forefront of attempts to convert buses to run on gas produced by
burning anthracite whilst the bus was in motion. With suitable
modifications, including changing the compression ratio, both
diesel and petrol engines could use gas. Initially the gas-
producer units were mounted on trailers towed behind the bus,
the law being changed to permit PSVs to tow trailers for this
purpose. ENOC received 36 trailers from a large batch built by
Bristol, and it is believed that 38 buses were converted, a mix of
AEC Regals, Leyland Tigers and Titans and Dennis Lancets.
The experiment was centred on Maldon depot in 1941, despite
some routes there needing to climb one of the steepest hills in
Essex — Market Hill. 'Producer gas' buses were generally
reckoned to be underpowered, and most of ENOC's conversions
involved single-deckers, unlike the more extensive operation
by London Transport with ST-type double-deckers. Maldon
depot was chosen probably because it had ample space to

accommodate the trailers and associated paraphernalia, as well as for its proximity to Morison's office in Chelmsford. Interestingly, LT also embraced Morison's technology and based its first large-scale gas operation at Grays — the nearest suitable garage to ENOC's works in Chelmsford.

Producer-gas operation never reached the Government's target of 10% of all buses in the larger operators' fleets but did spawn one further experiment, in the form of ENOC's 3874, whose Bristol registration (HHT 459) gave a clue as to its origins. Bristol Tramways built a specially modified L-type chassis, with extended wheelbase and an overall length of 30ft (against the maximum permitted of 27ft 6in for two-axle single-deckers). The extra 2ft 6in accommodated an integral gas unit housed in an enclosed compartment at the rear of the ECW body, which, unusually for ENOC, had a forward entrance. With a larger fuel hopper than before, the L6GG (**L** type **6**-cylinder **G**ardner **G**as) was expected to be able to cover 150 miles before refuelling and servicing. Describing the bus in mid-1942, *Passenger Transport Journal* explained how 'the producer compartment is

completely insulated from the body by asbestos sheeting with a view to eliminating fire risk and possibly fumes. Double doors [at the rear] enable the producer to be reached for fire pricking, coaling or ash dropping'. Despite acclaim in the trade press of the day, 3874 and Eastern Counties' similar LE1 remained unique in their respective fleets and were later converted to conventional operation, fitted with standard Gardner 5LW engines and reduced to 27ft 6in length by ECW in 1946. With the added complexity and attention that producer-gas buses required, it was not surprising that operations were quietly dropped as soon as the fuel situation had improved.

Despite the problems of wartime production, ENOC was fortunate to receive some new vehicles every year from 1940 onwards. It actually received more standard and 'unfrozen' models early on in the war than the later utility models, in contrast to the experience of many big operators. First to arrive, in 1940/1, were 25 ECW-bodied K5G 'deckers. Although these were ostensibly identical, the first 10 came from ECW's factory at Lowestoft before it was abruptly shut down in May 1940 amid fears of

an invasion. ECW then relocated to an unused United Counties garage at Irthlingborough in Northamptonshire, whence the other 15 buses followed between August 1940 and February 1941. A further 25 Bristol L-type single-deckers on order were cancelled.

In 1942, other than the producer-gas Bristol L described above, ENOC received only five new buses. Two were on 'unfrozen' Bristol K5G chassis, but the others were Guy Arabs, and all five had utility bodies — by Duple and Brush. The utility-bus programme had been devised jointly by the Ministry of Supply and the Ministry of War Transport and involved a selected group of manufacturers' producing vehicles to a rigid specification designed for ease of construction by relatively unskilled workers and avoiding the use of scarce resources such as aluminium (which was needed for aircraft production). The Ministry of War Transport allocated vehicles as it saw fit, often wrecking operators' attempts at standardisation, and ENOC was thus lucky to be allocated only one new chassis type and three body manufacturers, as 1943's deliveries comprised a further seven Arabs, all with Brush bodies.

As well as the limited supply of new buses, a number of vehicles were rebodied and introduced more variety in the form of East Lancs bodies — 11 'deckers and one saloon. In all, over 30 buses were rebodied, but far more extensive was the rebuilding programme, designed to extend the lives of buses that would otherwise have been withdrawn, and to deal with wartime damage. Beadle secured the lion's share of the work, rebuilding more than 130 bodies during the war; such was the scale of the problem that at least three Lancets were each rebuilt three times! ECW also contributed a small number of rebuilt bodies, while much work was undertaken in the company's own workshops.

With the reduction in traffic in some areas, ENOC was able to loan a small number of saloons to London Transport in 1940/1 to help bolster the latter's Blitz-ravaged fleet. However, ENOC was to suffer its own losses as a result of enemy bombing, by far the worst being in May 1943, when a direct hit on Chelmsford garage destroyed 25 buses. Chelmsford had a number of factories engaged on important wartime work and hence was a natural target for German bombers; vehicles were subsequently dispersed to a number of parking grounds at night, to reduce the risk. Ironically, one of the more tragic incidents occurred in the Midland Section in what might today be called 'friendly fire': a Leyland TD4 'decker on the Luton–Hitchin road unwittingly drew up behind a US Army lorry carrying bombs; the lorry had caught fire and blew up almost immediately, virtually destroying the bus and killing three passengers.

In 1944 only one new bus was delivered, but it was particularly significant and thankfully is still with us today, albeit awaiting 're-restoration'. No 3885, (JVW 430) is a Bristol K5G with the prototype postwar ECW body and was used for a while as a demonstrator. The following year brought four more Bristol K5Gs, with chassis numbered in the utility range but with postwar ECW bodies; the 1946 deliveries — three Ks and 13 L single-deckers — came on a mix of wartime and postwar chassis. More unusual deliveries in 1945/6 were solitary examples of an interesting concept, the Beadle chassisless single-decker, but their story really belongs to the next chapter, as we examine the boom years of the late 1940s — and the change of ownership that was to shape the rest of the company's future.

4. Nationalisation and Standardisation

The immediate postwar years were to prove difficult for the company. Traffic levels were buoyant and passenger expectations high, yet new vehicles and materials to repair the war-ravaged fleet were in short supply. Fuel shortages continued for a while, but, by the spring of 1946, services were starting to return to normal. Sunday-morning buses were restored in March, and the following month the former Hillman's service once again reached Bow. Some express services were also resumed, while in Clacton some prewar services were restored in readiness for the expected influx of summer visitors. The rest followed in 1947, and by 1948 the remaining coastal summer express services had all resumed.

With fuel still on ration for private motoring, ENOC sometimes struggled to cope with the traffic on offer. New buses were still scarce and mostly followed prewar practice, albeit with some updating of body styles. More revolutionary were the two Beadle chassisless saloons delivered in 1945/6. As explained in the last chapter, Beadle had rebuilt a significant number of buses for ENOC during the war. However, the Dartford company had also been busy with aircraft production and realised the potential for using aluminium extrusions to build a strong but light body. (After initial experiments in 1947/8 ECW would also turn to aluminium framing, in contrast to most other traditional bus bodybuilders.) Beadle's prototype bus was delivered to ENOC in 1945, its integral body fitted with a Commer petrol engine, later replaced by a Gardner 4LW diesel. Another followed in 1946, this time with a Bedford engine and running units recovered from a scrapped former Southern National vehicle. The full-fronted bodies looked far more sleek and modern than the half-cab Bristol Ls being delivered at the same time, but, despite this, only nine more Bedford-Beadles were bought (in 1949), and the Bristol/ECW dominance was not seriously challenged.

There was an element of dual sourcing in 1947's new-vehicle intake, as much out of necessity (to renew the fleet as quickly as possible) as of choice. The 61 buses and coaches included the inevitable ECW-bodied K and L types, but more unusual were 18 Leyland PD1 Titans, also bodied at Lowestoft. The classic Bedford OB appeared in two forms, as Beadle buses and Duple coaches, the latter looking just like the thousands that were to

enter service with small operators all over the country. In the late 1940s ECW would also be kept busy rebodying mid-'30s GO and K 'deckers, some of which also received the more modern and lower PV2 radiator, improving their appearance considerably. Some prewar Leyland Titans were similarly rebodied at this time.

Deliveries in 1948 saw Bristol and ECW in total dominance, with 37 new vehicles. Most were K-type 'deckers, including a quartet which introduced Bristol's own six-cylinder AVW engine to the fleet, but there were half a dozen Ls, split equally between express (dual-purpose) and bus versions. Not all entered service directly with ENOC, however, and, to understand why, we need to consider the change of ownership that was to determine the company's entire future.

We saw earlier how ENOC came to be owned 50% by Thomas Tilling Ltd, 25% by the London, Midland & Scottish Railway and 25% by the London & North Eastern Railway, giving the company a stable and secure footing that enabled it to expand and consolidate its position as Britain emerged from the Great

The control room and clock at Chelmsford's bus station look down on a wonderful single-deck contrast *c*1950. Dennis Lancet 3482 (AVW 460) of 1934 looks dated alongside 3923 (HKK 26), the prototype Beadle-Commer lightweight chassisless bus, new in 1945. The latter lasted only until 1956 — just four years after the Lancet was withdrawn. *Charles F. Klapper collection, courtesy The Omnibus Society*

Depression at the start of the 1930s.
However, World War 2 had a serious
impact on the finances of the railway
companies in particular, and the 1945
General Election brought the Labour
party to power with a mandate for
change. Thus the scene was set for a
radical change in the ownership of
public transport. Nationalisation of the
railways was seen as inevitable, if not
exactly welcomed by the shareholders
in the existing 'big four'. Attitudes in
the bus industry were rather more
mixed. The industry was in effect split
into four sectors: the Tilling Group, the
BET (British Electric Traction) group,
the municipally owned undertakings
and the independent sector. A fifth force
was the London Passenger Transport
Board, established in 1933 and
providing what some saw as a role-
model for responsible, efficient
planning and delivery of public
transport. The Tilling/BET joint venture, T&BAT, had been
dissolved in 1942, and the two groups now had radically
different views. For BET, nationalisation would come only over
its dead body — certainly over the dead body of Managing
Director John Spencer Wills. Tilling's Sir Frederick Heaton took
a very different view. During the war he had advocated a national
transport authority based partly on the principles behind the
LPTB, with a series of 'Area Boards'. Meanwhile, the municipal
sector was already publicly owned but under local-government
control and fiercely opposed to central-government interference,
while the independent sector cherished that independence,
although some might subsequently look avariciously at the
compensation paid to the road hauliers which were compulsorily
bought out to form British Road Services.

Labour's manifesto pledge evolved into the 1947 Transport
Act, and so from 1 January 1948 the railway companies were
nationalised and placed under the control of the newly formed
British Transport Commission (BTC). Thus a half share in
Eastern National became Government property, but Tilling
remained in effective control, as it had been since 1931.
Sir Frederick Heaton took a pragmatic approach and opened

negotiations with the Government, leading to the sale of the whole of the Tilling Group to the BTC in the autumn of 1948, much to the disgust of BET, which remained privately owned. Thus ENOC was now fully nationalised and would remain so for the remainder of our 'glory days' and, indeed, for almost 40 years.

And so back to the fate of some of those shiny new Bristol Ks of 1948. London Transport had also come under BTC control and was, like everyone else in the industry, desperately short of serviceable buses, so a deal was struck whereby 180 new Tilling Group buses would be diverted to LT and released to their rightful owners later. ENOC's contribution comprised a baker's dozen from the 1948/9 orders — K types 4000-7 and 4030-4 — the last not being delivered to ENOC until June 1950.

Fleet renewal continued in 1949 with 40 new vehicles and yet more elderly buses rebodied. A pair of OB buses were accompanied by another half dozen Duple coaches on the same chassis (although the coaches were stored until 1950), along with the nine Beadle buses incorporating Bedford running units. Seven Ls and 13 Ks completed the picture, to close arguably the most turbulent decade in the company's history.

The first half of the 1950s was to see a series of far-reaching acquisitions and disposals that would finally define ENOC's territory. Most will be recounted in the following three chapters, but first we must start the decade on its very first day, with the takeover of the long-established Hicks Bros Ltd of Braintree. Hicks' history dated back to 1913, and that company had built up a substantial business, with depots in Braintree and Silver End and routes extending to Chelmsford, Bishops Stortford and Witham, plus express services to Clacton and London. Strictly speaking, Hicks was sold to the BTC, not Eastern National, but was placed under ENOC control in a similar way to Borough Services in the 1930s. Hicks' vehicles were gradually repainted from their dignified royal blue and yellow into the equally dignified Tilling green and cream, and vehicles from the main ENOC fleet were drafted in as the old Hicks stock was gradually phased out. Full integration came in 1954/5, as will be described later.

At the time of the BTC takeover the Hicks fleet comprised 48 buses and coaches, but these were maintained as a separate fleet and only 22 survived to receive ENOC fleetnumbers in 1954; they were not actually transferred to the 'parent' fleet until 1955. These survivors ranged from a pair of 1931 Leyland Lion saloons and six prewar Titans (which had originated with the Bolton and Wallasey municipalities or Ribble) through to more modern

ECW contrast. Late-1940s deliveries comprised a mix of Bristol K5Gs and Leyland PD1s with near-identical lowbridge ECW bodies, slightly tidied up as compared to the 1944 prototype — note the sliding windows, for example. Ready to depart for Chelmsford from opposite directions are K5G 3964 (MPU 25) at Southend Victoria station and PD1 3983 (MPU 44) in Braintree bus park; both would be withdrawn in the mid-1960s. *Kevin Lane collection; Frank Church*

The 1950 takeover of Hicks Bros plugged an important gap in ENOC's territory and brought with it a lengthy service into central London. During the period when Hicks was managed as a separate company, 90 (OVW 756), a Strachans-bodied Guy Arab III of 1949, departs the 'temporary' King's Cross Coach Station on its 2½-hour trip via Tottenham, Epping and Dunmow. The bus became ENOC 1191 in the 1954 numbering and lasted until 1959, being sold then to Moore Bros and re-entering the ENOC fleet in 1963, rebodied and disguised as JVW 999! *Andy Meadows collection, courtesy Chris Stewart*

The Hicks service became ENOC route 322 and for many years was operated by Bristol KSWs fitted with platform doors, but in 1961 MW bus 502 (1266 EV) was in charge, complete with smart side route-boards, at the Euston terminus used from 1954 until ENOC took over the new Tillings coach station at King's Cross, opened in 1963. *P. J. Relf*

By way of contrast, ENOC also ran its own express service (B) from King's Cross to Braintree and Halstead, but by a completely different route — via Stratford, Ilford, Romford, Brentwood and Chelmsford. Dual-purpose-seated Bristol L5G 3971 (MPU 32) represents the competition. *Richard Delahoy collection*

postwar rolling stock that included a pair of all-Leyland PD1s (later converted to open-toppers) and 10 Guy Arabs, all but two being lowbridge 'deckers; a 1947 Leyland PS1 bus and a 1949 Austin CXB coach completed the picture. In something of an anomaly, three buses ordered by Hicks but delivered after the sale to the BTC — an impressive full-fronted Maudslay Marathon III coach and a pair of Strachans-bodied Guy Arabs — were allocated ENOC numbers 4108-10 on delivery and were painted in Tilling colours but did not form part of the ENOC fleet at that time. The other 26 Hicks vehicles culled between 1950 and 1954 comprised a mixed bag of types but with a predominance of second-hand Leyland Tigers and Titans. Hicks also had a business running tours and excursions from Clacton, which the family retained with six vehicles as Cansdall Coaches Ltd.

The early 1950s saw further, relatively minor service changes and new routes introduced, while the renewal and standardisation of the fleet marched on relentlessly — until the acquisitions to be recounted in Chapter 7 reintroduced a degree of variety. In 1950 there arrived 56 new vehicles and four second-hand. During the year the 'box' dimensions in the Construction & Use Regulations were finally relaxed to permit 30ft-long single-deckers on two axles, so that an initial 13 35-seat Bristol Ls built to the old length were followed by 11 of the longer LL type, offering four more seats but still with the traditional rear entrance. Much more modern-looking and luxurious were 10 short Ls with full-fronted ECW full-coach bodies, often referred to as 'Queen Marys'. These were ENOC's first heavyweight postwar coaches and were accompanied by five lightweight Bedford OBs, the last to be purchased new. One of the 'Queen Marys', 4107 (PTW 110), is preserved by the Eastern National Preservation Group; a familiar sight on the rally scene in the 1970s and 1980s, it is currently receiving its second full restoration.

Almost overshadowed by the single-deck influx were 17 Ks to the old 26ft x 7ft 6in dimensions, followed by seven 27ft KSs. By 1951, however, full advantage was being taken of the

newly permitted 8ft width. Thus of the 46 brand-new buses delivered in '51 — no coaches this time — seven of the LLs were narrow chassis fitted with wider bodies, but the remaining 11 were long *and* wide LWL types; 28 KSWs redressed the balance in favour of the double-decker. One oddity was 3850 (TTW 268), with a contemporary registration but with a much older fleetnumber (new vehicles at this time being numbered in the 40xx and 41xx series); it was in fact based on the chassis of 1948 K type 4005, which suffered severe accident damage in 1951. Most unusually, 4005's *body* was retained and fitted with a brand-new *chassis*; the damaged chassis then being rehabilitated and fitted with an 8ft-wide body on the 7ft 6in chassis frame! The cause of standardisation was not helped by the purchase from the Brighton, Hove & District fleet of four elderly AEC Regents rebodied by ECW or Beadle during the war. These were bought for conversion to open-top, allowing ENOC to reintroduce open-top seafront services at Clacton; Westcliff was then running similar services in Southend, also with ex BH&D Regents, plus Bristol GOs.

At this stage it is worth considering liveries. From National days in the early 1920s, buses were painted grey; this was changed to red and white in 1923, but in 1928 the livery changed again in Essex (but not in Bedfordshire!), mainly on single-deckers, to green with white relief. Thus at the outset the fleet was in a state of transition, green taking over in both areas by the end of 1931. The basic scheme comprised mid-green, relieved by three dark-green bands, with a white roof and window surrounds; in some cases the roof was also green. Coaches tended to be in a reverse scheme with greater use of dark green. Tilling influence brought lining-out and black beading between the various colours, with cream replacing white. Gradually this was simplified, whilst during the war many buses were painted dark grey, as colour pigments became unobtainable and labour could not be spared for anything other than the simplest application. Postwar the familiar style of Tilling green with cream window surrounds for

In 1950 four Brighton, Hove & District AEC Regents dating from 1932 were acquired and converted to open-top; No 102 (GW 6263) fails to attract any custom for its trip from Holland-on-Sea through Clacton to Jaywick Sands. Later numbered 1158, it was replaced in 1958 by a converted Leyland PD1. *Charles F. Klapper collection, courtesy The Omnibus Society*

single-deckers (later a cream band below the windows) or two cream bands for double-deckers, set off by black lining, wings and mudguards, was the standard right through until the NBC era. Coaches were predominantly cream, with green relief (or, in the case of the Queen Marys, polished side mouldings) and green wings/mudguards.

To anyone who has grown up in an era where prices increase regularly, it is perhaps astonishing to reflect that ENOC had not increased its fares since 1933. However, the relentless rise in operating costs could no longer be absorbed by increased passenger numbers, and in 1951 an application was made to the Traffic Commissioner for an increase — fares being as tightly regulated as were routes and timetables. Permission was eventually granted for increases of ½d for fares up to 6d, 1d on fares up to 1/- and so on (the decimal equivalent being an increase of 0.21p up to 2.5p, 0.42p up to 5p, etc). The table gives some examples of the outstanding value that even these increased fares offered.

Before moving on to more momentous events in the early 1950s, however, we need to retrace our steps to the formation of ENOC and to the southwestern corner of the territory, to understand the muddle that was Grays.

Route	From	To	Journey time	Single fare	Decimal equivalent
14A/B	Melbourne Estate	Chelmsford station	8 minutes	2d	1p
104/6	Clacton bus station	Little Clacton	10 minutes	5d	2p
23/A	Braintree	Halstead	30 minutes	8d	3½p
53B	Luton	Whipsnade Zoo	38 minutes	1/-	5p
1	Chelmsford	Maldon	43 minutes	1/-	5p
18	Colchester	Halstead	50 minutes	1/4	7p
34	Bedford	St Neots	85 minutes	1/9	9p
104/6	Clacton bus station	Dovercourt	1 hour	2/-	10p
10	Chelmsford	Bow	90 minutes	2/8	13½p
17	Bedford	Aylesbury	2 hours	3/2	16p
19/A	Clacton	Southend	3½ hours	5/6	27½p
51	Tilbury Ferry	Harwich	4¼ hours	6/8	33½p

F
537

THE
LICENSING AUTHORITY
FOR PUBLIC SERVICE VEHICLES
EASTERN TRAFFIC AREA

NOTICES

AND

PROCEEDINGS

No. 537

Monday, June 4th, 1951

Communications should be addressed to the Clerk to the Licensing Authority for Public Service Vehicles, Eastern Traffic Area, Sussex House, Hobson Street, Cambridge, and postage must be prepaid.

Telephone Nos.: Cambridge 3211-3.   Telegraphic Address: "Transco," Cambridge.

The Office of the Licensing Authority is open for Public Business from 10 a.m. to 4 p.m. from Monday to Friday, and from 9.30 a.m. to 11.30 a.m. on Saturday.

D. VARIATION OF CONDITIONS ATTACHED TO ROAD SERVICE LICENCES

F./R.20/—**The Eastern National Omnibus Co. Ltd.**, New Writtle Street, Chelmsford.
Application is made to vary the conditions attached to the respective Road Service Licences and Backings for the stage services as detailed on Schedule "A" as follows:—

Proposals for Increases in Stage Carriage Fares

(a) Single fares (all services)—

Present fare.	Proposed fare.	Present fare.	Proposed fare.
2½d.	3d.	4½d.	5d.
3½d.	4d.	5½d.	6d.

(b) Return fares (all services)—

Present fare.	Increased by.	Present fare.	Increased by.
2½d., 3½d., 4½d. & 5½d.	½d.	2/- to 3/6	3d.
7d. to 11d.	½d.	3/7 and upwards	4d.
1/- to 1/11	1d.		
	2d.		

(c) Adults' and scholars' weekly tickets.
An increase of 10% on existing rates.
No weekly tickets to be issued where the revised adult single fare is less than 4d.

(d) Adults' and scholars' season tickets.
An increase of 10% on existing rates.
No season tickets to be issued where the revised adult single fare is less than 4d.

5. All Change at Grays

We saw in the Prologue how from 1921 National came to operate services in the 'London Country Area' on behalf of the London General Omnibus Co. The agreement had established three territories — the Metropolitan Police district, (within which National would not run at all), the London Country Area (where National would operate services on the LGOC's behalf, using buses and premises rented from them), and the National Company's Area (where National would be free to operate as it chose, and the LGOC would not run at all). The boundary between the Country Area and the National's 'freehold' territory ran through Bishops Stortford, Harlow, North Weald and Brentwood, then due south towards the Ockendons before turning sharply to the west to pass between Rainham (LGOC) and Aveley (National). Interestingly, at this point the London Country Area was only about two miles wide; elsewhere the

distance between the boundaries of the Metropolitan Police area and National's area was up to 20 miles.

Significantly, the territorial carve-up placed Grays firmly in the National territory, but a number of natural traffic objectives, such as Rainham, Upminster and Hornchurch, lay inside the London Country Area. National had established its first operations in Grays in 1921 and opened a proper garage there in 1924. Services were developed locally within the Grays/Purfleet/Tilbury area and to adjacent towns and villages. From 1928 the Upminster service (40) was also extended to Romford, nominally jointly with the LGOC, as it penetrated deep into the 'Country' area. However, local services in the Grays area were to prove a serious problem for National; the local council freely licensed anyone who wanted to run a bus service, and National faced intense competition from a plethora of local operators

using small, fast buses and with a less
disciplined approach to adherence to
timetables. The situation did not
improve through the decade, and it was
pointless trying to buy out the
competition, as new competitors could
simply start up the next day.

The consequence was that Grays was
the only National depot not to make a
profit. Further complicating matters
were the fact that the LNER (unlike the
LMS, which operated the local rail
services) had little interest in the area
covered by Grays garage's operations,
and the fact that some of the routes
operated into the London Country Area.
As a result, Grays garage remained with
the National company initially and was
not transferred to ENOC until October
1930, by which time agreement had
been reached that its future did indeed lie as part of ENOC.
By then the 1930 Road Traffic Act had been passed and would
shortly bring order to the chaos experienced in Grays, allowing
operations there to be put on a more stable and profitable basis.
Immediately prior to the Act's coming into effect, almost 50
separate operators had been identified in the area; three years
later this had been reduced to six. This cull came about as some
simply did not bother to apply for licences, others were refused
and some gave up or had their licences revoked. ENOC also
started to acquire some of the competition in 1933.

A much more ominous change would result from the
legislation that established London Transport (more properly
the London Passenger Transport Board), from 1 July 1933.
This re-drew the territorial boundary, moving it eastwards to
bisect Grays. The area west of the town centre was designated
as part of the LPTB 'Special Area', within which LT had a legal
monopoly of bus services, and the boundary northwards was
defined by the route of the aforementioned service 40, which
passed to LT and later became the 370. The result was that, from
31 August that year, all the services terminated in the town
centre, LT working to the west and ENOC to the east. The only
exception was the 38 to Purfleet, which remained with ENOC
until the following April, allowing LT to acquire seven other
operators on that route. In return, ENOC acquired the eastern
ends of a number of services that LT had taken over through
its powers of compulsory purchase within the Special Area,
including the Great Yarmouth summer express service of Tilbury
Coaching Services. ENOC also bought out further small
operators to rationalise operations, although some independents
remained. More significantly, Westcliff-on-Sea Motor Services
and Borough Services both reached Grays on their competing
services from Southend. The Borough service became an ENOC
route in 1940, as explained in Chapter 2.

So far as the fleet was concerned, ENOC transferred four
Gilford single-deck buses and the solitary Guy FCX three-axle
'decker to LT, with which they lasted until 1935. Conversely,
none of the independents' vehicles joined the ENOC fleet, except
for three coaches that came with the business of Stanford Motors
of Stanford-le-Hope in 1935.

The changes left a simple but totally unsatisfactory situation,
all services being forced to terminate in Grays town centre and
passengers compelled to change buses on their way to work or
to visit friends and relatives. This was surely not what those
who drafted the LPTB legislation had intended, but for locals
it was to be a sad fact of life for the next two decades. The only
exception would be the Green Line service to London, which
started in ENOC territory at Tilbury but was not allowed to carry
local traffic there.

The interim: from September 1951 until February 1952, LT operated the former ENOC routes with a mix of ENOC buses and its own STLs. Incongruously carrying London Transport fleetnames and stencil-holders on their Tilling green livery, single-deck Bristols 3721 (FNO 794), a 1937 JO5G, and 3898 (KNO 601), a 1946 L5G, contrast with red STL500 (AYV 688), seen heading deep into rural south Essex at Linford. *D. W. K. Jones; W. J. Haynes; Richard Delahoy collection*

The aftermath: with ENOC now reduced to just an operator of long-distance services, 1935 Bristol GO5G 3639 (DEV 475) prepares to depart for Southend on the former Borough service 70 as a green RT waits time on the other side of the road on the 370 to Romford, which incorporated the former ENOC 37A from Tilbury Ferry. *London Trolleybus Preservation Society*

We can now fast-forward to the early 1950s, to see how, with ENOC and LT both in state ownership, a solution was found. The Road Passenger Executive within the BTC was tasked with addressing the overlapping or anomalous territories of a number of its constituent undertakings and duly considered the wholly unsatisfactory situation in Grays. The outcome was an agreement whereby the local ENOC services in the Grays area would be transferred to LT and through services restored across the town centre. The first stage was implemented in September 1951, when ENOC acquired the last remaining independent, Our Bus. Then, on the 30th, LT took over the operation of ENOC's garage in Argent Street, along with 13 services. These continued to be operated by the former ENOC buses, transferred to LT and running in Tilling green but with London Transport fleetnames. Twenty-eight buses were transferred, the single-deck contingent comprising five Dennis Lancets, six Bristol JOs, five Bristol Ls (including 3874, the former producer-gas bus), and a pair of Bedford OBs, while 10 utility-bodied Guy Arab 'deckers completed the group. The transfer did *not* include half a dozen new K types recently allocated there, as they were transferred away from Grays the day before LT took over. In their place (and to avoid having to use the OBs and Lancets), LT transferred in 14 of its own standard STL-class AEC Regent 'deckers in full Central Area red livery.

For the next three months this interesting assortment of buses operated the routes unchanged. Then, from 2 January 1952, a complete route revision was implemented, restoring cross-town services. All the former ENOC buses were returned to the company, along with the Argent Street depot building, standard LT Country Area buses thereafter running all the services from LT's own garage in London Road. ENOC used Argent Street for a while to store withdrawn vehicles but sold the building in 1954. LT buses were now to be seen running deep into south Essex, firstly to serve the community of East Tilbury but also to get workers to the large Bata shoe factory there and to the oil refineries at Coryton and Shell Haven — points due south of Chelmsford.

ENOC would henceforth be only a minor player in the area, with routes from Tilbury Ferry (a popular crossing-point in the days before the Dartford Tunnel was opened in 1964 and still the lowest public crossing of the Thames) and Grays to Brentwood, Chelmsford, Harwich and Clacton, and from Grays to Southend, jointly with Westcliff. Services were also provided to Bata's at East Tilbury from Stanford-le-Hope and Laindon. And so ends — or almost ends — the complex story of Grays, a town divided. It only remains to note that, from 1964, ENOC strayed a little into LT's territory again with the 153 that ran via Chadwell St Mary *en route* to Tilbury Ferry, albeit with a restriction to prevent ENOC abstracting LT's valuable local traffic.

Yet more changes have taken place in more recent and less glorious years, and it is perhaps ironic to note that ENOC's successor, First Essex, provides an important cross-town link with the 100, running through the town centre on a flagship route from Chelmsford to the massive Lakeside Shopping Centre, west of Grays. Meanwhile, LT's eventual successor in the area, Arriva, has retreated significantly, and some independents have re-entered the market; one has since disappeared, after its licence was revoked. *Plus ça change …*

6. 'Midland National'

Once again, to understand the dramatic changes that took place in 1952, we need to go back to the 1920s and to the operator that never was — 'Midland National'. As explained earlier, National only became involved in Bedfordshire by chance. The LGOC had operated buses in Bedford before World War 1, but the vehicles and premises there were requisitioned by the Army. By the time the garage was returned to the LGOC after the war, operations there would have breached a territorial understanding that the LGOC had reached with the British Electric Traction group (BET). However, Bedford was to prove a good negotiating pawn, as the LGOC was keen to persuade National to leave London and needed something to offer in return; that something was Bedford. A deal was cut whereby National would take over the garage and would in return withdraw the last of its steam buses based at Peckham and Putney. National duly commenced operations in Bedford in August 1919, recruiting General's former local manager Mr Kishere to run the depot.

From these small beginnings were to grow a business that would finally break away from its National roots in 1952, taking with it half the fleet — some 239 operational buses and coaches.

Expansion followed through the 1920s, so that, by the time the National company was divided to facilitate the investment by the 'big four' railway companies, buses were being operated over a large territory stretching from Northampton, in the northwest, through the heartland of Bedford and Luton eastwards into Hertfordshire and northeastwards to St Neots, Cambridge and Huntingdon. There is not space here to recount the full story of that expansion, but suffice to say it was achieved partly by opening up new routes and bases and partly by acquisition, the most significant being Road Motors of Luton (with 14 routes and 40 buses); other takeovers had included St Ives & District, Biggleswader Blue Services and the Progress Bus Co of Huntingdon.

The southern boundary of the operations was set by the London Country Area agreement with the LGOC, in the same way as it was for Grays. Indeed, the Road Motors services south from Luton were latterly operated on behalf of the LGOC and passed to what became the Country Area of LT in 1933. Within Luton itself, National was in competition with the municipal tramway, opened in 1908. We will return there in a short while, but first back to the railway investment. It had been intended to split National into four area companies, with each of the 'big four' railway companies taking a 50% stake in the appropriate National company. However, the LMS and LNER both had a significant presence in the area of the planned 'Midland National', and no sensible split could be determined. Equally, although most of Essex was LNER land, the LMS had an important interest in the south of the county as owner of the former London, Tilbury & Southend Railway. Hence a

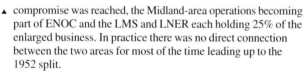

A deserted Whipsnade Zoo is the setting for 3707 (FEV 176), a Brush-bodied Leyland TD5 dating from 1937. Rebodied postwar by ECW, in 1952 it passed to United Counties as that company's 570.
Charles F. Klapper collection, courtesy The Omnibus Society

▲ compromise was reached, the Midland-area operations becoming part of ENOC and the LMS and LNER each holding 25% of the enlarged business. In practice there was no direct connection between the two areas for most of the time leading up to the 1952 split.

Early signs of the railway involvement in ENOC included an inter-available road/rail ticket between Bedford and Cambridge and the replacement of the Somersham–Ramsey LNER branch line by ENOC bus 39, worked by Huntingdon depot. Further road/rail tickets were subsequently introduced and bus services extended to terminate at railway stations in Leighton Buzzard, Dunstable, Rushden and Northampton, for instance. Expansion followed through the 1930s by the usual combination of acquisitions and the development of new routes. ENOC did not always have things its own way, however, with Birch Bros developing routes around Bedford and Rushden, as well as a London–Bedford express coach service that would later be operated by distinctive full-fronted double-deckers, before itself selling its bus operations, including the London services, to United Counties in 1968/9.

More ENOC buses were to be found in Cambridge through the 1931 takeover of Ashwell & District, the service becoming jointly operated with the Ortona Motor Co, one of the

constituents of Eastern Counties. By 1934, however, ENOC was running the Hitchin– and Bedford–Cambridge services alone, outstationing some buses in the ECOC garage there. Meanwhile the municipal tramway in Luton, opened in 1908, had become very run-down, and the Corporation approached ENOC to run bus services instead, for a guaranteed annual sum. That scheme did not meet with favour locally or with the Ministry of Transport, and instead, in 1932, Luton sought licences for its own bus services. Needless to say, these attracted objections from ENOC and London General Country Services. Negotiation followed and led to the signing, later in 1932, of a 21-year agreement between ENOC and Luton Corporation, defining their respective territories and allowing the Corporation to operate beyond its boundaries, to Dunstable and Houghton Regis. The following year there were various route swaps and rationalisations between the Corporation (which had bought out the Union Jack company), ENOC and LT.

Elsewhere, ENOC's territory was to be affected by the formation of London Transport and the consequences of LT's powers of compulsory purchase of operators within its area, some of which had extensive operations outside LT's area. One interesting deal involved ENOC's buying the Aylesbury Omnibus Co in May 1933 but then splitting that company's operations, various parts passing to London Transport, Thames Valley, City of Oxford and United Counties. The last had, like ENOC, come under Tilling control in 1931, and this was to lead to the transfer of most of ENOC's operations at Stony Stratford to UCOC, along with the depot there, in a portent of what was to follow 19 years later. Of the Aylesbury company's fleet, 17 joined the ENOC fleet, including a dozen recent Leyland Tiger coaches, four soon passing on to UCOC; a further six Tigers were not used by ENOC but went straight to City of Oxford and Thames Valley.

ENOC also benefited from LT's takeover of Strawhatter Coaches of Luton: LT took Strawhatter's London service but had no powers to run the summer express services to Bournemouth, Southsea, Margate or Great Yarmouth, and these duly passed to ENOC, along with eight modern Strachans-bodied Gilford coaches. A further purchase was of the Union Jack business. As described above, Luton Corporation had bought out this business, only for the owner, A. F. England, to start up again by buying other operators in Luton and Bedford! This time it was ENOC's turn to get out the cheque book, six vehicles joining the fleet as a result. Another payment brought the bus services of

Taylor of Meppershall, near Hitchin, although that firm's excursions and tours licences went to arch rival Birch Bros. Further north, ENOC consolidated its position in the north after United Counties acquired Meadows & Son of Barton Seagrave, near Kettering, but then passed the easterly routes and five buses to ENOC in 1939.

With the stability afforded by the Road Traffic Act's licensing system, ENOC invested in its premises in the Midland Section just as it did in the Eastern. A new bus station was provided in Bedford, the garages there and at Luton were rebuilt, and brand-new depot buildings were provided in Aylesbury, Hitchin and Huntingdon. Other investment included the allocation of all 25 Bristol K5Gs delivered in 1940/1 (3820-44) to the Midland Section. This was perhaps appropriate, as a number had been built nearby, at ECW's temporary wartime factory at Irthlingborough.

World War 2 brought similar problems to the Midland Section as it did to the Eastern, especially with the heavy traffic to factories at Luton and Dunstable. One further acquisition involved Gammond's Blue Coach service, from Bedford to Oxford. Gammond had previously resisted all offers to buy him out but decided to retire in 1941 and was on the point of selling to Red & White when Tilling and BET stepped in. A deal was struck for ENOC, United Counties and City of Oxford to buy the business jointly, with Oxford running it. This started in 1942, but the following year

Amidst postwar prefabs and new building work in Leagrave on the 57 to Luton (LMR) station is 3731 (FPU 511), the first ECW-bodied Bristol K in the fleet. It was rebodied just before transfer to United Counties and, after seven years with UCOC, passed to Thames Valley for a further six years' service. *V. C. Jones, courtesy Kevin Lane*

Another ECW-bodied K, the former ENOC 3809 (GTW 890) of 1938, represents the post-takeover scene. As United Counties 642 it stands in Biggleswade Market Square on the 176 to Sandy and Bedford, which had been numbered 8 in ENOC days. *Richard Delahoy collection*

In 1940/1 ENOC belatedly took delivery of 25 ECW-bodied Ks to normal peacetime standards; all were allocated to the Midland Section and remained there, passing into United Counties ownership in 1952. ENOC 3838 (JEV 429) would become UCOC 690.
A. M. Wright / Ian Allan Library

ENOC took over the operations. A further extension in the south in 1942 took ENOC buses well into LT Country territory, on the jointly operated Aylesbury–Great Missenden–Amersham route 369, created by extending an existing ENOC service over part of a withdrawn Green Line one.

The desire to improve and extend services in the Luton area had, over the years, strained the 1932 territorial agreement between ENOC and the Corporation, leading to delays in the traffic courts as applications were considered. To solve these problems and to achieve more efficient operations, the two parties entered into discussions after the war, resulting in the signing in October 1948 of a Luton & District Transport Co-ordination agreement. Within a defined area, which extended to include Whipsnade Zoo, Toddington and Streatley, ENOC and the Corporation each agreed to operate 50% of the mileage, with revenue being pooled and shared. This still left LT providing services to the south of the town, but there was no artificial division in the town centre in the way that Grays had been partitioned. (Jumping ahead a long way, the Co-ordination agreement would last until January 1970, when the Corporation sold out to United Counties.) The Luton scheme commenced on 1 January 1949, but the main benefits were not seen until

September, when a major revision and rationalisation of routes provided more cross-town services and simplified the network from 32 to 22 routes, achieving useful cost savings as well as offering a better service to the public.

And so to the big split. We have already seen (in Chapter 5) how, with all parties under state control, the messy situation in Grays was finally resolved. ENOC's Midland Section could hardly have been considered a mess, but it was an oddity. Almost entirely divorced from the Eastern Section, it had more in common with its northern BTC sister, United Counties (UCOC), even running into that company's headquarters town of Northampton. Perceived wisdom at the time considered that around 500 vehicles was the optimum size for a nationalised company to make best use of administrative resources, yet UCOC operated only around 300. ENOC was much closer to the optimum size, but its southerly BTC neighbour, Westcliff-on-Sea Motor Services, was also 'too small'. The solution was obvious — transfer the Midland Section to UCOC and merge it fully with that company, giving it the required critical mass, and transfer Westcliff to ENOC, to restore ENOC's size and put the whole of south Essex under the control of one company. The latter process will be described in the next chapter, but, to remain with 'Midland National' for the present, the change took place on 1 May 1952. UCOC took over 239 operational buses and coaches, an assortment of service vehicles, seven garages and seven outstations, operating over 110 bus routes and nine summer express coach services, the net value of the transferred business being £619,529.

In his history of United Counties, Roger Warwick notes that 'there seems little doubt that Eastern National engineered their fleet disposition over the months preceding the transfer to ensure that a greater proportion of elderly vehicles would pass to United Counties than a just allocation would have allowed'! The actual vehicles transferred ranged from 1930 Leyland Lions which dated back — just — to the old National company to brand-new Bristol LWLs and KSWs delivered only six months previously. They received new fleetnumbers in the range 101-883, to fit in with the indigenous UCOC fleet that had itself been renumbered in March 1952 in anticipation. The services, meanwhile, continued to use their ENOC numbers for a further year, until a comprehensive renumbering exercise was undertaken in March 1953.

Thus the operator that never was, 'Midland National', leaves our story, to become part of UCOC's own glory days.

▲ Also representing the United Counties era, former ENOC 4001 (NNO 101) backs off the stand at Kingsbury Square, Aylesbury, alongside an RT sold by London Transport to Red Rover of Aylesbury. The conductor is dutifully waving the bus back but has neglected to change the destination blind, so we cannot tell if this is a 366 to Halton Camp or the infrequent 368 to Stoke Mandeville Hospital — presumably the former, if the intermediate destination of Wendover is to be believed.
Richard Delahoy collection

▲ Conversion for driver-training duties can considerably prolong the lives of redundant buses. Bristol L5G KNO 603, new as ENOC 3900 in 1946, lingered on for eight years as a trainer with United Counties following its withdrawal from normal service in 1961. *T. M. Smith / Richard Delahoy collection*

City contributed a modern fleet of Leyland Titans, including LD7 (NVX 304), setting off from Wood Green 'coach station' in Lordship Lane; 2 hours and 37 minutes later it should pull into Southend's Tylers Avenue garage. Waiting there to return to London is LD24 (FJN 205), one of six all-Leyland PD2s ordered by City but delivered to Westcliff after the takeover. Roberts-bodied LD7 became ENOC 1124 and lasted until 1963; LD24 was numbered 1139, then 2119, and survived until 1965. Duple-bodied Leyland Tiger LT36 (DUC 912) of 1937, partly obscured by the taxi, did not survive into ENOC ownership, in contrast to a dozen of its sisters. *(both) Roy Marshall, courtesy The Omnibus Society*

7. South Essex Domination

After our jaunt around the south Midlands we must return to south Essex to put in place the final parts of the ENOC jigsaw. We have previously seen that ENOC's presence there was somewhat limited. In Southend the Corporation had abandoned its trams in 1942 but was running a significant fleet of buses and trolleybuses within the confines of the Borough boundary; the main operator in the area was Tilling (and later BTC) subsidiary Westcliff-on-Sea Motor Services, which in the 1930s had absorbed a number of competitors such as Edwards Hall Motors of Eastwood, Rayleigh Motor Services, Thundersley, Hadleigh & District, Rochford & District and Shoeburyness Motor Services. However, the linked businesses — Benfleet & District and Canvey & District — owned by the Bridge family meant that Westcliff did not have a monopoly on the busy A13 corridor or any presence at all on the expanding Canvey Island.

The other major route westwards out of Southend, via Rayleigh, Wickford and Billericay was well served by the Brentwood-based City Coach Co, its London (Kentish Town/Wood Green)–Southend route going back to 1927 and the days of New Empress Saloons. City had used much of the proceeds from the compulsory acquisition by LT of its London bus operations to set up a new head office and depot in Brentwood. Several local operators were acquired, including Laindon-based Tom Webster's Old Tom business. Laindon was to form part of Basildon New Town, as was Pitsea, with its own small operator, Campbells. Westcliff's trunk routes 2/2A/2B to Grays and Romford passed through the area; the Grays service (2) was joint with ENOC, which numbered its journeys as route 70.

Attempts at rationalisation in earlier years had been thwarted, Southend Corporation having rejected Tilling's approach in 1935 and the independent (non-Tilling) bus operators having successfully opposed a planned 1946 co-ordination agreement between Westcliff, Southend and ENOC. Interestingly, that agreement would have given trolleybus-running powers to the company operators, but it was not to be, and instead Westcliff and the Corporation had to be content with much more limited co-operation on a couple of town services. Once again, nationalisation was the catalyst for a solution. Seeing the writing on the wall, the Bridge family sold their bus interests to the BTC in 1951, and City followed in 1952; pending full rationalisation in south Essex, their vehicles and operations were taken over by Westcliff. Talks could now resume with Southend, where the trolleybuses were now less attractive to the Council, following nationalisation of the electricity supply industry. A far-reaching co-ordination scheme came into effect from 2 January 1955 and covered an area of almost 100 square miles, taking in what are now the districts of Castle Point and Rochford as well as Southend itself. Within that area, services were to be operated as Southend & District Joint Services, with the Corporation operating 37% of the mileage and the enlarged ENOC (incorporating Westcliff) 63%. Southend had abandoned its trolleybuses in October 1954 in anticipation, and the agreement would last until deregulation in October 1986.

As anticipated above, the precursor was for Westcliff (with City and Benfleet/Canvey) to be absorbed into ENOC, along with Hicks, and this took place at the beginning of 1955. With so many changes, ENOC's fleet-numbering system was in need of a radical overhaul, especially as Westcliff

City single-deck contrasts: Duple-bodied Tiger coach LS4 (LHK 415) gained ENOC coach livery as 126 and ran until 1961; it is seen in Victoria Coach Station, perhaps ready for relief duty on the express service D to Southend — note Bristol LS bus 405 (832 CVX) behind. Definitely *not* coaches were the half dozen Plaxton-bodied Seddon Mk IVs like 220 (OEV 408), formerly City S1, on a Brentwood local service. Dating from 1949, all had gone by 1961. *Kevin Lane collection; Michael Dryhurst*

had not used numbers at all. With the 1953/4 deliveries ENOC's numbers had exceeded 4200, all buses being numbered in one long series. In July 1954 a comprehensive renumbering took place, including all the (to be) acquired vehicles, using separate series to distinguish between single- and double-deckers.

An unfortunate consequence of the takeovers was the reintroduction of variety into a fleet that was fast standardising on Bristol/ECW products. Westcliff's stock of just over 140 vehicles was pretty familiar, thanks to the Tilling influence from 1935 on, albeit with plenty of elderly AEC Regent 'deckers and some Regal coaches, but the same could not be said of the others'. City contributed a largely Leyland fleet, including prewar three-axle Tigers and Gnus (the latter with twin-steering front axles) and postwar Tigers and Titans; delivered after the takeover were more Titans and underfloor-engined Royal Tigers. Seven Daimler CVD6s completed the double-deck fleet. More exotic were seven Commer Q4s and six Seddon Mk IVs, which shared small bus duties with 10 Mulliner-bodied Bedford OBs. Fourteen OB coaches completed the City contingent. The Benfleet/Canvey contribution comprised 21 utility Daimler CWs, many of which had come second-hand from Birmingham City Transport in 1949/50, plus three prewar Regents. The Hicks fleet was described in Chapter 4.

Liveries also presented an eclectic mix. Westcliff had used Tilling red/cream, City brown and cream, Benfleet/Canvey sage green/cream and Hicks royal blue/yellow. Through the early 1950s repaints had all been into standard Tilling green and cream but with Westcliff, Hicks or City names. Meanwhile, standard ENOC buses were loaned to Westcliff and Hicks and acquired a similar mix of names.

Returning to the Southend Co-ordination Agreement, services continued largely unchanged for the first six months, although the operation of many routes was swapped between the two parties to even out operating costs, Westcliff routes having higher average speeds and fewer stops than the Corporation's. In May 1955 the first upheaval took place, linking together shorter routes to provide more cross-town services — a process continued in subsequent years and aided by the replacement of Benfleet station level-crossing by an underpass, making it possible to run through services onto Canvey Island from 1962.

Westcliff also brought with it an important coaching business with considerable goodwill. There was a clutch of express services, including one to London ('numbered' D by ENOC, later X10 and finally 400) and other seasonal routes to the South

Westcliff rules: with Westcliff fleetnames disguising their origins, a contrasting pair of Daimlers. First, lowbridge Roberts-bodied CVD6 NVX 172, once City D2 but now carrying ENOC number 1217, heads down Southend High Street, pursued by a Corporation utility CWA6. Another Utility is former Benfleet & District FOP 417, one of a large batch of highbridge ex-Birmingham examples bought by Benfleet/Canvey in 1949/50. Seen at the Leigh Beck terminus on Canvey, it later passed to Southend Corporation.
Dennis Gill; J. F. Higham / Richard Delahoy collection

Southend's seasonal seafront services have not always been the preserve of open-top 'deckers. Bristol JO5G saloon JN 8567 of 1937 was one of a number of single-deckers in coach livery for the Kursaal–Leigh service, numbered 19/19A until the 1955 co-ordination scheme saw this changed to 67/68, to avoid duplication with ENOC's 19/19A from Southend to Clacton. Photographed in September 1949, the bus survived until 1959, latterly as ENOC 248. *J. C. Gillham / Richard Delahoy collection*

Westcliff's more modern stock fitted easily into ENOC's fleet, even if vehicles did need to swap Tilling red for green. Bristol LWL5G bus EJN 635 of 1951 waits in Broadway Market, Southend, ready to depart for Wallasea Bay. Obsolescence rather than old age saw it withdrawn in 1965; latterly it had been ENOC 1134. *Richard Delahoy collection*

Westcliff's contribution to ENOC included a large depot and works at Prittlewell in Southend, whose skills will be called for in repairing 2502 (1847 F). The Lodekka had come to grief while working route 28, worked by Southend Corporation trolleybuses prior to the co-ordination scheme. *Richard Delahoy collection*

Campbell's of Pitsea contributed an assortment of buses but, more importantly, cleared the way for ENOC to monopolise operations in the area of Basildon New Town. Waiting time at Pitsea station in August 1949 is KNO 53, a 1946 Albion CX13 with a Pickering bus body, which took ENOC fleetnumber 001 when acquired in 1956; along with the entire Campbell's bus fleet, it was withdrawn later the same year. *Phil Picken / Richard Delahoy collection*

Coast acquired by Westcliff from Multiways during the war, when the latter had its fleet requisitioned. Westcliff was also famous for its extended tours, picking up in London as well as locally, and the Westcliff name was retained by ENOC for such operations into the early 1960s.

The final small operator in the area to pass to ENOC was Campbell's Motor Services of Pitsea, which had started life with horse-drawn wagons in the early part of the century. The business expanded in the 1920s and secured road-service licences under the 1930 Act, protecting its position around Pitsea. ENOC had only passed through the area on the longer-distance routes but opened a small base in Bull Road, Vange, in 1952, following the transfer of Grays depot to LT. Meanwhile, as the area to the north of Pitsea and Laindon started to be developed into Basildon New Town, turning acres of fields into a town eventually home to 100,000-plus people, Westcliff succeeded in obtaining licences for routes into the emerging town centre. The Campbell brothers decided to retire, and their services and 10 vehicles passed to ENOC in 1956, leaving the way clear for ENOC to monopolise the New Town as it expanded. That expansion was to be one of the few promising developments of the late 1950s and 1960s, as we shall see shortly. In the north of the county, a similar New Town at Harlow offered less scope for ENOC, as it fell within LT territory.

8. The 1950s — The Tide Starts to Turn

We have seen how the shape of ENOC changed quite dramatically between 1950 and 1955. Just as the fleet numbering needed sorting out, so did the route numbers, to eliminate duplication. A comprehensive scheme was effected in 1955, built around the existing Southend-area numbers, by allocating blocks of numbers to various areas — thus Chelmsford services were numbered between 30 and 59, Colchester took 70-89, Maldon 90-99, and Clacton 100 upwards. A big gap followed until 231-6 for the ex-Campbells routes, 241-50 for Basildon, 251 up for Brentwood (251 itself being allocated to the former City Southend–Wood Green service) and finally 300 onwards for Bishops Stortford, Braintree and Halstead. Later, limited-stop services took 400 upwards, and coach services, previously lettered, became X-numbered in 1962.

New vehicle deliveries through the 1950s followed a *very* predictable pattern, reflecting developments by Bristol and ECW, with the move to underfloor-engined saloons and the introduction of the revolutionary Bristol Lodekka, offering a normal seating layout on both decks in place of the

four-abreast seating upstairs, with a sunken gangway (which also served to inconvenience those downstairs), that had characterised the lowbridge layout since the late 1920s. The Lodekka offered an attractive and spacious bus yet was only 13ft 5in high. Many parts of ENOC's territory needed low-height buses, nowhere more so than in Chelmsford itself, where the railway bridge adjacent to the bus station/depot offers only 14ft clearance, and a number of depots were also inaccessible to conventional full-height (14ft 6in) 'deckers.

The switch to the underfloor-engined LS came in 1952/3, the bus and dual-purpose versions initially having dual (front and *rear*) doors, although the rear entrances were all removed by 1960. LD-type Lodekkas supplanted KSWs as the standard 'decker from 1954 and continued the mix of five-cylinder Gardner and six-cylinder Bristol engines. The LS ('Light Saloon') integral was replaced by the MW ('Medium Weight') chassis — still with ECW bodywork, naturally — during 1957. Whether LS or MW, ENOC's policy was to specify five-cylinder

In 1950 both Westcliff and ENOC took Bristol L coaches with luxurious full-fronted ECW bodies for extended tour work — PTW 101-10 for ENOC (as 4098-4107) and EHJ 27-9 for Westcliff. Now with ENOC (as 324) but exploiting the goodwill carried by the Westcliff name, EHJ 29 loads in Victoria Coach Station for a tour. Most lasted until 1963. *Richard Delahoy collection*

1954's pair of prototype Bristol SCs were followed by 20 production models like 451 (9575 F), delivered in 1958 and seen here at Wilson's Corner, Brentwood, in September 1961. All were withdrawn by 1964 and thus escaped that year's renumbering, although 451 was allocated 1008 in the new series. *D. Savage / Richard Delahoy collection*

Gardners for buses, for fuel economy, but the more powerful 6HLW in coaches. In the search for further economy, in the face of rising costs and declining traffic, ENOC also took both prototype Bristol SCs in 1954 and then 20 production examples in 1957/8, replacing many of the early postwar Beadle chassis-less buses and bus-bodied Bedford OBs. The SCs featured the small Gardner 4LK engine (except for one prototype, initially fitted with a Perkins P6) and were reported to return 20mpg. A more unusual experiment involved LS bus 400 (476 BEV), which ran with a Commer TS3 engine for around six years and must have sounded *very* strange!

Following the upheavals of the early part of the decade, the remainder of the 1950s were to prove almost boring, relieved by the takeover of Rose Bros (Primrose Coaches) of Chelmsford in 1958, with an express service to Great Yarmouth. The solitary coach acquired from Rose was a 1951 Thurgood-bodied Leyland Royal Tiger.

Many factors conspired to start the downward spiral in which the bus industry found itself at this time. Increasing car ownership, rising operating costs, changing social habits and the growth of stay-at-home entertainment in front of the (black & white) TV all hit ENOC. Yet most of the fleet was still crew-operated, although from 1956 onwards most LS and MW saloons were converted to OMO (one-*man*-operated, in those politically-incorrect days!), but none of the traditional half-cab rear-entrance single-deck buses was rebuilt to front-entrance and hence remained crew-operated until the last were withdrawn in 1965. The Suez crisis forced fuel rationing to be introduced in January 1957, only adding to the problems, but one bright spot in May that year was a major reconstruction and extension of the Central Works in Chelmsford. On a site in New Writtle Street occupied continuously since World War 1, the expanded building of 46,000sq ft could handle 18 vehicles on heavy overhaul at any time and was home to 150 employees. The fleet at that time was almost 700 strong, and overhauls were undertaken every 50,000 miles. 'New Writtle Street' was a familiar address, as it appeared on the side of every ENOC bus and coach to record the location of the company's head office.

An interesting expansion in coaching activities saw the introduction of a 'Coach/Air' service from London's Victoria Coach Station and the Euston Square coach terminal (replaced in 1963 by a new King's Cross coach station) to Southend Airport for a variety of continental European destinations. Indeed, the development of coach services was a high-spot of the period.

Bristol MW contrast: brand-new 488 (1252 EV) stands outside ECW's Lowestoft factory, with sister 489 behind. They were part of a batch of seven dual-purpose MWs delivered in 1959 with full coach seats in a bus-shell body fitted for one-man operation. The full-coach equivalent is represented by 483 (282 NHK) at Lower Rock Gardens, Brighton, in May 1961. In the 1964 renumbering 488 would become 1404 and 483 would take 335, the renumbering creating discrete blocks of numbers for different types. *Richard Delahoy collection; Peter Relf*

The standard double-decker changed from the lowbridge Bristol KSW to the low-height LD Lodekka in 1953/4; 1355 (SHK 522) in Chelmsford bus station represents the old order, 1496 (267 GVW) at Southend Victoria the new. The former City Coach Co Wood Green–Southend service, numbered 251 by ENOC, was repeatedly restocked with the newest buses in the fleet and had a peak vehicle requirement of over 20 buses to maintain a quarter-hourly headway.
(both) Richard Delahoy collection

As well as the ex-BH&D Regents at Clacton, a further three Tilling-bodied examples came from the same source in 1954 for open-top use in Southend, but these lasted only until 1957.
No 1008 (GJ 2011) leaves the Thames Drive terminus at Leigh in July 1956.
Frank Church

▲ In a posed press photograph taken on 15 May 1957, the new paint shop in the expanded Central Works at Chelmsford is home to an unidentified prewar Bristol L, Lodekka 1523 (81 JNO), Tillings LS coach PYO 758 (only two years old and set to join the ENOC fleet in 1965) and LS bus 397 (473 BEV). Hand-painting produced a superb finish, and the fleet remained very well turned out, even into the 1970s. *Ian Allan Library*

9. The 1960s — An Uphill Struggle

And so to the final decade of this review of ENOC's glorious years. It has to be said that the glory was fading fast as the decade progressed. The downward spiral that began somewhere around the mid-1950s continued, with a relentless rise in operating costs, staff shortages and declining traffic, leading to service cuts and rising fares, leading to declining traffic, leading to … well, you've got the picture. Some economies could be made through increased use of one-man-operated buses, and by the end of the decade these were replacing even crew 'deckers. One-man operation of 'deckers came shortly after the first Bristol VRs arrived in 1969, but, conversely, there were still a few crew-operated *single*-deckers in use. Thankfully, the decade was spared the more extreme cost-cutting that would later see many depots closed. Meanwhile, the expansion of Basildon was to prove one high-point, a new garage opening in 1961 in Cherrydown — conveniently just the other side of the railway line from the bus station — to replace the temporary Bull Lane site in Vange.

Most acquisition possibilities had by now been exhausted, but there were some small opportunities and a far more significant one. The small ones saw ENOC buy the services of two operators in Colchester — Mmes Mawdsley & Brown in 1960 and George Digby the following year — and Wright Bros of Harlow in 1962. Far more significant was the 1963 purchase of the long-established Moore Bros of Kelvedon, bringing 12 coaches and 28 buses into the fleet. Moore's filled a large gap in ENOC's network in mid-Essex as well as providing a garage in Kelvedon, reintroducing the Guy Arab (with a further pair on order, delivered after the takeover) and introducing ENOC to the Commer Avenger coach. Even so, ENOC still did not have a monopoly in central Essex, as the 40-strong fleet of G. W. Osborne & Sons of Tollesbury remained stubbornly independent (finally passing to another independent, Hedingham Omnibuses, in 1997).

Further expansion occurred in 1962, when ENOC was given control of the Tillings Travel coach fleet, previously managed from London and used mainly on private hires and extended tours. The successor to National's London coaching interests of the 1920s, Tillings had used a distinctive livery of pearl grey with maroon wings, but this was gradually replaced by the standard cream/green of ENOC's own coach fleet, and vehicles were swapped from one fleet to the other quite regularly. Both ENOC's and Tillings' coaching activities would later form part of National Travel (South East) in 1974, ironically based in the former Moore's depot at Kelvedon, by then no longer used by ENOC.

The 1960s saw some major changes in the fleet, albeit through a process of evolution rather than revolution. Further relaxation of the Construction & Use Regulations permitted longer buses,

Moore Bros of Kelvedon was ENOC's last major acquisition in the glory days. The fleet consisted largely of Guy Arabs, in both single- and double-deck form. Duple-bodied LPU 940, seen in Colchester bus park in pre-takeover days, became ENOC 027 in 1963 but was withdrawn the same year, along with all the Moore's single-deck stock save for three Commer Avenger coaches. Some of the double-deckers survived much longer, the last not going until 1975.
Roy Marshall

and so the 60-seat LD Lodekka gave
way to the 70-seat, 30ft-long FLF
version in 1960. A solitary 70-seater
had joined the fleet in 1958, 1541
(236 LNO) being one of a pair of
prototype flat-floor Lodekkas
produced by Bristol and ECW in 1958,
but with a rear open platform in
contrast to the front-entrance FLF.

The single-deck fleet continued to
use 30ft Bristol MWs, in bus, dual-
purpose (coach seats in a bus shell)
and coach formats. However, Bristol's
revolutionary rear-engined chassis, the
RE, offered greater capacity, and
coach versions were taken in 1964 and
1968, but the bus version did not make
an appearance until the end of the
decade, the first 20 (of an eventual
fleet of 55) arriving in 1969. The RE
coaches were mainly conventional
ECW 47-seaters, including some with
bus doors and destination gear, but the
1968 deliveries included a quartet of
the very rare short RESH model with
comparatively uncommon (on Bristol
chassis) Duple Commander 36-seat
bodies for extended tours. Adding
more variety to the coaching stock
were half a dozen Duple-bodied
Bedford SBs, Tillings taking a further
six that would later join the ENOC
fleet; all had relatively short lives,
being withdrawn by 1970.

Other interesting coaches,
ultimately to number 15, were double-
deck FLFs. As loadings on Southend–
London service D increased, ENOC in
1962 took an initial three FLFs with 55
proper coach seats and a large luggage
area at the rear of the lower saloon.
These attractive and impressive
vehicles were later used on Coach/Air
services to Southend Airport and other

express services. The last five, like the final FLF buses, were the extended 31ft version, fitted with more powerful Gardner 6LX engine and semi-automatic gearbox — in this author's (biased!) opinion, amongst the finest buses ever built. The bus-seated 'semis' were used chiefly on the former City Coach Co 251 service and its 151/351 variants, leading to their starring role in the hugely successful 1960s and early '70s TV comedy series *On the Buses*, much of the filming taking place in Wood Green garage. The antics of Luxton & District's service 11 to Cemetery Gates are now available on video and are a wonderful reminder of the deliciously un-PC 1960s!

A further change to the fleet was another comprehensive renumbering, in August 1964, designed for the first time to group common types together, with coaches numbered in the hundreds, single-deck buses from 1000 upwards and double-deckers from 2000; different types were then given discrete blocks within the scheme (eg Bristol Ks 2200-70). This numbering scheme, suitably modified, is still used today by First Essex as successor to ENOC. The year also witnessed the single most comprehensive set of bus service revisions in the company's history, improving services in the Basildon area.

The open-top fleet was renewed in 1966 by the conversion of 10 Bristol KSWs of 1953; the extensive rebuilding included the complete removal of the sunken gangway, effectively converting them to highbridge layout. (Thankfully seven still survive, although none is in regular bus service.) They replaced the dozen ex-City and ex-Hicks PD1s that had been converted between 1956 and 1960 to replace the prewar Regents and Bristol GOs; one of the Titans is preserved.

The evolutionary changes to the fleet were concluded early in 1969 with the entry into service of the first five Bristol VRs. Initially in bus livery, most were quickly repainted into dual-

purpose colours and put to work on the X10, despite their standard bus seating. Their stay there was to be short-lived, but they represented the sea-change that was to come in the next decade, as OMO (or, more properly, one-*person*-operated) 'deckers swept into the fleet. Indeed, by the end of our glory days, all the half-cab saloons were long gone, as were the LS coaches and many LS buses. In the double-deck fleet, some of the newest KSWs remained, along with a few of the Moore's Guys, but it would not be long before even the first Bristol LDs were withdrawn. The fleet had perhaps reached the zenith of standardisation.

The success story of the decade was the expansion of ENOC's network of express coach services, partly by improving the long-established routes but also by opening up new territory such as the X28 (Southend–Cambridge) and X29 (Southend–Derby). The biggest opportunity came with the long-awaited opening in 1964 of the Dartford Tunnel, replacing the previous ferry crossing or detour into London. Jointly with East Kent, Maidstone & District and Southdown, ENOC introduced a new network, marketed as 'Dartford Tunnel Coachways'. Destinations included Southsea, Dover, Folkestone, Ramsgate and Hastings. Bus route 2 was also extended through the tunnel to Dartford in 1967. Meanwhile other expansion took ENOC coaches to the West Country, on services operated jointly with Bristol Greyhound and Royal Blue, and in 1967 the 'Essex Coast

In complete contrast (and most untypical of Tilling) were a dozen Bedford SBs with Duple coach bodies; half were new to ENOC and the other six came via Tillings Transport. In June 1965, a month after transfer, 507 (8 BXB) departs Basildon bus station on the summer-only X30 from Southend to Bognor Regis, one of the Dartford Tunnel Coachways services introduced the previous year. The Bedfords were all withdrawn in 1969/70. *W. T. Cansick / Richard Delahoy collection*

A start was made in 1962 to upgrade the Southend–London express service D (later X10) with purpose-built Bristol FLF coaches. Ultimately there were 15 of these superb vehicles, but they were later displaced by standard bus-seated VRs, in a bid to reduce costs. In happier days 2600 (184 XNO) leaves Basildon on the X8 variant that ran via Southend Airport; there was also an X7 from Canvey to London. The rear views show the luggage compartments of the standard and 31ft-long versions.
Richard Delahoy collection (main picture); W. T. Cansick

▲ Express' was set up as a pooled operation involving ENOC,
► Grey-Green and Suttons Coaches of Clacton. The similar 'East Anglian Express' started the following year, ENOC being joined by Eastern Counties and Grey-Green.

As has been mentioned earlier, the company had also inherited Westcliff's programme of extended tours and continued to use the Westcliff name until at least 1961. ENOC added its own programme of tours from mid- and north Essex, and in 1962 these were combined into one overall offering with 23 different tours. Later in the decade, tours were extended to France, Belgium and the Netherlands and ultimately across most of Europe.

While coaching developments probably represented the high points in a turbulent decade, the growth of Basildon New Town, where the population had grown six-fold in 20 years, helped to compensate for the declining traffic elsewhere.

The 1960s closed with yet another fundamental change in ENOC's ownership and direction. The BET group, faced with another Labour-inspired Transport Act, finally decided to sell out to the state at the end of 1967; the THC, of which ENOC formed a part, was then merged with BET's bus interests to form the National Bus Company, which took effect from 1 January 1969.

In practice, the major changes that NBC was to introduce did not take place until the 1970s and — in hindsight — were a major factor in ending the glory and traditions of companies like ENOC. Meanwhile, privatisation and deregulation, the two forces that were to turn the industry upside down in the late 1980s, could scarcely have been imagined in 1969.

Thus concludes our story covering four decades of proud service. Defining just when the 'glory days' ended is inevitably subjective, but the 1968 Act was a watershed and started a whole new phase in the history of companies like Eastern National. That is a story for another day.

FLF evolution: the 70-seat, forward-entrance Lodekka was the standard bus from 1960 until 1968, ENOC taking 232 plus the 15 coaches. Representing the earlier style is EOO 582, still numbered 1614 when caught leaving Southend on a well-loaded 251; later it became 2740. Later models lost the upper cream band, and the final 48 were 31ft long, with semi-automatic gearbox and the more powerful Gardner 6LX engine. No 2902 (WVX 529F) is seen at Basildon on the 151, a variant introduced in the 1964 revisions to improve services for the New Town.
Alan B. Cross; W. T. Cansick / L. F. Watson collection

Perhaps the greatest moment of fame for the 'semis' came with their starring role in *On the Buses*, the TV sitcom which brought us Stan, Jack and, of course, Blakey, the Inspector. No 2917 (AEV 811F) is blinded for Luxton & District's 11 to Cemetery Gates but is really in Prittlewell works yard.
Terry Coughlin / Richard Delahoy collection

Epilogue

The new order cometh: Bristol VRs 3000-4 (CPU 979-83G) were the forerunners of a large fleet of OMO 'deckers, but their initial entry into service was not without its troubles. There was resistance to one-manning such a large bus, while the DP livery did not fool passengers on the X10, upon which they replaced the FLF coaches. The VRs quickly reverted to bus routes, Maldon-allocated 3000 being seen almost grounding as it leaves Southend on its 3¼-hour marathon run across the county. A look back to the Introduction reveals the unmistakable affinity of body style with the K type, even if the engine has moved to the back!
Richard Delahoy collection

In a few words I will attempt to bring the story up to date. Two of the most obvious NBC influences were in the livery and the fleet. NBC imposed a rigorous centralised policy — in many ways no different from the Tilling style that lasted through the BTC/THC era — but somehow lacking the class. Buses and dual-purpose vehicles donned National green, thankfully often relieved by white, coaches becoming all-over white and then being hived off to form part of National Travel South East.

The all-conquering Leyland National supplanted the RE as the standard single-decker but in turn was usurped by the Lynx before the minibus revolution took full effect; small numbers of LHs, Ford R1014s and Bedford YMT and YMQS types also provided some variety. More recently the Dennis Dart has reigned supreme. Coaches returned to the fleet in the late 1970s, and the RELH gave way to Leyland's ubiquitous Leopard and then the Tiger, plus some more prosaic — and short-lived — MCW Metroliners, after which coaching activities were largely abandoned.

The double-deck fleet followed a more conventional path, the VR reigning supreme until superseded from 1981 by the Leyland Olympian, the latter including some DP and full-coach versions. However, 'deckers were by now very much a declining breed and today form only 13% of a fleet of around 350 vehicles, against 68% of 650 in 1969.

Universal one-person operation was not achieved until after the last FLFs were withdrawn in 1981. Other economies have seen most of the traditional ENOC depots closed or relocated; after many years of neglect, Chelmsford's garage and bus station are due to be replaced in 2003, and yet another link with the past will be lost. Deregulation spawned the emergence of many new, mostly small competitors and led to frequent, often destabilising changes to routes, yet many elements of the core ENOC network from the 1930s can still be traced today.

Inevitably, politics and economics have been the dominant influences. Partial deregulation from 1980 onwards had less impact than the more radical politicians had hoped, but that was more than compensated for by the 'big bang' of full deregulation and privatisation in 1986. Somewhat against the odds, ENOC's management argued successfully against splitting the company into the smaller units so beloved of the Conservative Government, bought the company as a management buy-out in 1986 but then sold it on to Badgerline in 1990, only for the latter promptly to split the company in two! Operations in south Essex, including some routes in north London operated under contract to London Transport (shades of the National/General arrangements of the 1920s!) became Thamesway, with a livery of yellow and brown (later pink). Badgerline subsequently merged with Grampian Regional Transport and metamorphosed into FirstGroup, which duly reunited the two halves but then spoiled the effect by finally dropping the Eastern National name, both as a fleetname and as the company's legal title. Hence today's successor to the Eastern National Omnibus Co Ltd, First Essex Buses Ltd, trades simply as 'First', and the fleet is rapidly losing all traces of its local identity as the corporate livery sweeps away the last vestiges of tradition.

▲ Chelmsford garage plays host to a fine line-up in March 1963. No 1138 (FJN 206), left, was a Leyland PD2 ordered by City but delivered to Westcliff in 1952 after City had sold out to the British Transport Commission. In the middle is a typical ENOC Bristol K/ECW, 1318 (ONO 51), which ran for London Transport for a year when brand-new in 1949. Completing the trio, 1108 (ENO 937) is a 1937 Leyland TD4 rebodied by ECW in 1949 and by now sporting a Gardner 5LW engine, Bristol gearbox and postwar Leyland radiator. All would be withdrawn by 1967. *Philip Wallis*

Two views of ex-Westcliff 1937 Bristol K5G 1254 (JN 9542) in Clacton bus station, accompanied in the first picture by 1271 (GNO 695), a year newer yet looking older, as it still has its prewar high-mounted radiator. Many former Westcliff 'deckers ended their days at the other end of the county, operating from Clacton depot; these two were withdrawn in 1959. *(both) Richard Delahoy collection*

Also ex-Westcliff, and posed outside the former Benfleet & District garage at Hadleigh (still used in 2003 by First Essex, the successor to Eastern National), 2253 (DHJ 610) was a 1949 Bristol K6B with the inevitable ECW lowbridge body. Delivered in Tilling red, it had gone green and had initially become 1325 in the ENOC fleet, assuming 2253 in the 1964 scheme. When photographed in March 1966 on an enthusiasts' visit it only had just over a year's service left. *Alan Osborne*

▲ No 297 (MPU 31) was a comparatively rare dual-purpose version of Bristol's standard L-type single-decker. New in 1947 as 3970, it ran until sale in 1962 to well-known dealer North's of Leeds. Nearing the end of its career with ENOC but still looking well cared for, it is seen working a Bishops Stortford town service. *Martin Weyell collection*

▲ Later front-engined saloons were longer Bristol LLs with classic
ECW 39-seat bodies, like 334 (RHK 127), seen in Chelmsford
in March 1963. The 8ft-wide body sits slightly uncomfortably
on a chassis designed for a 7ft 6in body! Numbered 4092 when
new in 1951, it was renumbered in 1954 and again, shortly before
withdrawal in 1964, as 1122. It later served with contractor
Seddon of Bolton. *Philip Wallis*

Leyland contrasts: MPU 48 was one of 18 PD1s delivered in 1947 when new buses were in short supply. At least its lowbridge ECW body was at home in the ENOC fleet. Having begun life as 3987, the bus was renumbered 1115 in 1954; it was sold in 1963, but not before it was caught in Braintree bus park. At the same spot and on the same route is FJN 202, one of the batch ordered by City but delivered to Westcliff. It arrived in 1952 in City brown as No LD2 but took ENOC number 1137 when absorbed along with the other Westcliff stock; in the 1964 renumbering scheme it became 2117. Both buses were sold to Twell, the Lincolnshire dealer who took many redundant ENOC buses in the mid-1960s. *(both) John Boylett*

In the immediate postwar period the City Coach Co had built up a substantial fleet of double-deckers for its busy Wood Green–Southend route, including 16 Leyland Titans of the PD1 and PD1A varieties, with bodies by Beadle, Alexander and Roberts. Colour shots of buses in City livery are particularly rare, but in 1952 Frank Church recorded LD5 (NVX 302), one of the 1948 Roberts-bodied PD1As, outside Wickford's Castle Hotel *en route* from Southend to London.
Frank Church

Nearing the end of its ENOC career as ENOC 1122, NVX 302 waits at Benfleet station on the short but busy 26A service to Canvey's Seaview Road. Between 1956 and 1960 10 of the City Titans were converted by ENOC to open-toppers, but 1122 retained its roof and was withdrawn in 1963.
Essex Bus Enthusiasts' Group collection

Also Roberts-bodied was City Daimler CVD6 D5 (NVX 175), one of a batch of six new in 1949. We are fortunate that Frank Church also photographed this bus in 1952 at the same location as LD5 opposite, as the pictures show contrasting City liveries, the Daimler being in the later, simplified version with less cream, introduced in 1951. *Frank Church*

Seen loading for the lengthy run to Grays, NVX 175 had become ENOC 1220 by the time this photograph was taken at Southend Victoria. The bus had a shorter-than-usual career, being ousted in 1962, when only 13 years old, by the march of Bristol/ECW standardisation. Would the driver prefer NVX's pre-selector gearbox to the more common but harder-to-master crash 'box found on the Bristols, one wonders? *Essex Bus Enthusiasts' Group collection*

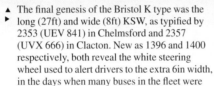

▲ The final genesis of the Bristol K type was the
► long (27ft) and wide (8ft) KSW, as typified by
2353 (UEV 841) in Chelmsford and 2357
(UVX 666) in Clacton. New as 1396 and 1400
respectively, both reveal the white steering
wheel used to alert drivers to the extra 6in width,
in the days when many buses in the fleet were
still to the old 7ft 6in limit in place until 1950.
The Essex registrations disguise the fact that
both were originally in the Westcliff fleet; both
were new in 1952 and lasted until October 1969,
when these 55-seat 'deckers were replaced by
new one-man-operated, 53-seat Bristol RE
single-deckers. *Photobus; John Boylett*

Three generations of open-toppers. Slowly gathering custom at the ENOC terminal at Jaywick Sands, 1244 (JN 8570) had in an earlier life plied on Southend seafront. Unusually it was new (in 1937) as an open-topper, being fitted with a roof in 1942 when seafront trips were not exactly in demand! It reverted to open-top configuration in 1949 and ran in Southend and Clacton until withdrawn in 1957.

Meanwhile, when John Boylett caught ex-City Leyland PD1A 2112 (NVX 313) in Clacton bus station in 1964 or 1965, he could little have realised that the KSW alongside, 2384 (WNO 480), would itself be decapitated for the 1966 season! 2384 still exists in 2003, under restoration by a preservationist in the Southend area. *Essex Bus Enthusiasts' Group collection; John Boylett*

SEE EAST ANGLIA BY EASTERN NATIONAL COACH

DAY TOURS TO CAMBRIDGE - NORWICH - BURY ST. EDMUNDS - FELIXSTOWE

ALDEBURGH - SANDRINGHAM - LOWESTOFT - YARMOUTH

APPLY COMPANY'S OFFICES - JACKSON ROAD OR PIER AVENUE - CLACTON-ON-SEA - PHONE CLACTON 944

EASTERN NATIONAL

HOLLAND-ON-SEA (FERNWOOD AVE.)

SEA FRONT SERVICE

LEYLAND

NVX 313

WNO 480

In all, a dozen early-postwar Leyland Titans acquired with the City and Hicks fleets were converted by ENOC to open-top between 1956 and 1961. One of a pair ex-Hicks with Leyland bodies converted in 1961 and which enjoyed surprisingly short (four-year) careers as open-toppers, 2104 (MNO 194) pauses at the Kursaal on the Leigh–Shoeburyness 68 service. *John Boylett*

Proving that the sun does not *always* shine in Southend, replacement Bristol KSW 2387 (WNO 485) has pulled up outside the gasworks; the crew stare seaward from the deserted upper deck. The gasworks bridge behind the bus was used to carry coke landed at the jetty into the works; it was demolished many years ago when the works closed. Southend's far more infamous low bridge, at the Pier, which required special operating procedures on seafront services to prevent passengers from being decapitated, was demolished early in 2003 and replaced by a new, higher structure. *R. L. Wilson collection / Photobus*

Eastern National operated two versions of the so-called 'Queen Mary' style of ECW coach body, exposed-radiator examples on Bristol L chassis — some new to ENOC or Westcliff and others bought from United Counties in 1958 — being joined in 1961/2/3 by 10 concealed-radiator LL6G models new to Tillings Transport. Seen in Cambridge in August 1963 as ENOC 020, MXB 748 was one of the Tilling specimens, while former Westcliff EHJ 28 reminds us that in the 1960s many buses and coaches passed to contractors (in this case, Clugston of Scunthorpe) for works transport. Thankfully PTW 110, one of those new to Eastern National, has survived and is currently being restored for a second time. *Philip Wallis; Richard Delahoy collection*

Although it also looks superficially like a 'Queen Mary' coach, the axles and wheels of this vehicle reveal a quite different beast — an AEC Matador acquired from the RAF in June 1959 and fitted with a body built in ENOC's Central Works incorporating parts from ex-Tilling coach MXB 738. Later numbered 0101, it was usually to be found parked in a corner of Chelmsford garage, making occasional forays on its trade plates to recover failed buses. *Alan Osborne*

Bristol's first move into underfloor-engined single-deckers produced the LS, ENOC and Westcliff between them taking 48 bus examples, some initially fitted with dual doors. Seen at Victoria Coach Station, 1859 F, with its pre-1964 number (441), is hardly the most attractive vehicle for the London–Southend express service. Sister 1860 F, carrying its 1964 number (1245), looks more at home laying over in Braintree; the LS alongside, 476 BEV, was also new to Eastern National but passed in 1966 to Hedingham & District, which was steadily expanding and is now a major force in north Essex. *(both) Photobus*

The standard ENOC 'decker in the mid-1950s was Bristol's revolutionary Lodekka. One of the first was 1434 (XVX 20), seen in later life as 2403 after it had lost its rather ugly 'long apron' front in favour of the later, more refined version. Neither the bus nor Maldon depot, where it was photographed in 1966, remain, although sister 1431 (XVX 19) is preserved by the Eastern National Preservation Group.

John Boylett

Loading in the middle of the road is most definitely not allowed in Chelmsford bus station in 2003 but was an accepted fact of life 40 years earlier, when Lodekka 1521 (79 JNO) was taking on a good load on the former Hicks service to Braintree and Halstead — service 311, not 31 as the camera angle might suggest; the 31 would have picked up on the opposite side, for Maldon! The bus would become 2490 and would enjoy an 18-year life, finally being replaced by a Leyland National in 1975. *Philip Wallis*

▲ The LD Lodekka was revolutionary in offering low height with a conventional gangway upstairs but achieved this by using a dished gangway in the lower saloon. Bristol and ECW subsequently refined the design to give a totally flat floor downstairs. One of a pair of prototypes produced in 1958, and initially used as demonstrator, 1541 (236 LNO) was ENOC's only rear-entrance 30ft Lodekka. Renumbered 2510, it spent much of its life at Brentwood, being seen here at the former City depot in North Road. This bus is now preserved. *Alan Osborne*

SERVICES

11 & 11A SOUTHEND — CHELMSFORD

FREQUENT DAILY SERVICE

WITH CONNECTIONS FOR: ONGAR, HARLOW, BISHOPS STORTFORD, DUNMOW, BRAINTREE, HALSTEAD, ETC.

EASTERN NATIONAL

PRIVATE

CAUTION

62 FPU

▲ The LD ceased production in 1960, being replaced by the F series, and ENOC's final two 60-seaters appeared as FS models rather than LDs. Nos 1569/70 (61/2 PPU) frequently seemed to be used as driver trainers, the latter being seen in later life as 2539 at Southend depot. *Alan Osborne*

▲ The Bristol SC was an attempt at producing a lightweight, economical one-man-operated bus for quieter routes but did not enjoy a long life in the ENOC fleet. No 450 (9574 F) was one of six delivered in 1958, joining 16 others already in the fleet. All had been withdrawn by 1964, none lasting long enough to use the 10xx series allocated in the 1964 renumbering scheme; 450 would have become 1007. The bus is seen in an unusually quiet Clacton bus station.
Essex Bus Enthusiasts' Group collection

In bus form the Bristol LS was akin to a brick on wheels, but thankfully the coach version showed more subtlety in its design, even if it had an old-fashioned outward-opening door and a wind-down windscreen. ENOC received its first coach models in 1953, but Westcliff was a year ahead, taking nine in 1952 and another pair in 1953. In an almost deserted Victoria Coach Station, FJN 165 stands in front of what appears to be a Lydney-bodied Guy Arab UF of South Midland. The LS was numbered 370 when the Westcliff fleet was absorbed into ENOC, becoming 310 in 1964 before withdrawal the following year.
Essex Bus Enthusiasts' Group collection

FJN165

For the Bristol MW, ECW introduced a more raked front on the bus-shell body. Displaying ENOC's shortest destination, Harwich-based 1303 (1865 F), new as 461, shows a comparatively rare livery variation with cream window surrounds; most MW buses had a cream band below the windows and green surrounds. The dual-purpose (coach seats in a bus shell) variant used the half-green, half-cream livery carried by Halstead-based 1432 (JHK 456C), seen loading in Braintree on the ex-Hicks London service.
Alan Osborne; Photobus

Another of the dual-purpose MWs, 1426 (MOO 178) basks in the Chelmsford sunshine before returning to its home base of Basildon in the late 1960s. A 1962 delivery as 565, it adopted its new identity in 1964, the bus MWs being numbered in the 13xx series, the DPs from 1400. The PAYE board in the windscreen is probably a recent addition, as the vehicle was not fitted for OMO until as late as 1966. It lasted until 1976 and retained coach seats to the end, unlike many of its sisters, which were given bus seats (often removed from LD Lodekkas) in the early 1970s.
Richard Delahoy collection

◄ Once Tillings Transport, the London-based coach operation, came under ENOC control there were frequent transfers between the fleets. VYO 768, a 1959 MW coach, became ENOC 381 in 1965 and is seen posed outside Maldon depot in 1966 on an enthusiasts' visit. Red fleetnumber and depot-allocation plates were a feature of the 1964 numbering scheme, to distinguish them from the black plates of the previous (1954) number series.
Alan Osborne

MU4454

Eastern National
Omnibus Co.,
Ltd.

STAGE TRIP CODE CLASS FARE

SINGLE

▲
◄ It was rare for buses to run for long without advertisements, but four-month-old 1627 (JWC 713) had managed to avoid being disfigured when photographed in Chelmsford on the offside loading platform (the crew no doubt still in the canteen). By contrast 1647 (VWC 50), seen *c*1966 as 2770, was one of a number of FLFs to receive illuminated advertisement panels on the offside; note the conductor counting cash on the pavement at Victoria Circus in Southend before continuing the journey from Canvey to Shoebury. The whole area was about to be razed to the ground, to be replaced by a modern (1960s-style) shopping centre.
Philip Wallis; John Boylett

The 1963 takeover of
Moore's of Kelvedon added
new interest to a fleet
reaching the peak of
standardisation. The single-
deck bus fleet of Guy Arabs
did not see the year out and
remained in Moore's colours,
like KGT 379, seen in
Colchester bus station in
March 1963, six weeks after
the takeover, now displaying
ENOC fleetnumber 032,
KN (Kelvedon) depot plate
and 'EASTERN NATIONAL
SERVICE 71' poster in the front
window. The double-deck
Arab fleet lasted longer,
some being almost new,
like 372 WPU seen in
Chelmsford, also in March
1963, and most receiving
ENOC livery. Indeed, the last,
including a pair delivered
new to ENOC after the
takeover, were withdrawn
only in 1975. Happily, sister
bus 373 WPU is preserved.
(both) Philip Wallis

Moore's also contributed three rare Commer Avenger coaches, including 7652 VW, a Yeates-bodied Avenger IV model dating from 1960. Initially numbered 039, it was used as the Colchester United FC team coach, becoming 102 in 1964. In ENOC livery and by now allocated to Clacton, it was photographed leaving Victoria for Jaywick Sands in September 1967. *Alan Osborne*

An earlier unusual coach was KKX 408, a Duple-bodied Leyland Tiger PS1 of 1947, acquired in 1951 with the business of Queens Park Coaches of Halton, near Aylesbury. Allocated fleetnumber L128 by ENOC (it is not clear what the 'L' stood for), it passed to United Counties in 1952 as part of the transfer of the Midland Section, only to return to ENOC in 1958 with a number of other UCOC coaches.

This time numbered 014, it was painted in ENOC coach colours and ran until 1962.
Richard Delahoy collection

▲ Later FLF deliveries had a simplified livery, with the
▶ upper cream band omitted as a economy measure.
These two pictures also illustrate the difference
between the standard 30ft model, exemplified by
2878 (SVX 277D) at Victoria Circus, Southend, and
the 31ft model, such as 2894 (WNO 982F) at Benfleet
station, with longer rear bay. Both feature the Cave-
Browne-Cave heating/ventilation system, which
replaced the conventional radiator and required
large thermostatically controlled shutters either side
of the destination display. No 2878 ran with ENOC
for only five years, being one of 15 swapped in 1971
for Bristol VRs in the Alexander (Midland) fleet
in Scotland. This presaged the later and more
extensive NBC/SBG exchanges.
Alan Osborne; Richard Delahoy collection

▲ Two shots of the wonderful FLF coaches at work on
◄ the Southend–London express services, X7/8/10.
The unmistakable surroundings of Victoria Coach
Station provide a backdrop for 2607 (BVX 669B),
seen when new in 1964 but already renumbered
from 1672 in the renumbering scheme implemented
that August. In contrast, a well-loaded 2614

(AVX 975G) pulls away from Basildon bus station
on the Canvey–London X7 *c*1969. The five semi-
automatic, 31ft-long examples carried both this full
coach livery and the half-and-half DP livery at
different times in their short lives as coaches;
all were rebuilt as buses in the 1970s.
Richard Delahoy collection

EASTERN NATIONAL
Express Coach Service **X10**

SOUTHEND
Westcliff
Leigh
Hadleigh
South Benfleet
Pitsea
Vange
BASILDON
Gidea Park
Romford
Newbury Park
Snaresbrook
Leyton
Dalston
Islington
LONDON

TIMES & FARES
1964/65 from
5th OCTOBER, 1964
until 14th APRIL, 1965

ALL TICKETS ISSUED ON THE COACHES

▲ ECW introduced a radical change to the MW coach
◀ body in 1961, replacing the familiar raked frontal
style of 329 (7015 HK), a 1958 model new as 456,
with a much more upright but rounded style as
shown by 357 (12 DLY), a 1962 Tilling delivery
transferred to ENOC in 1963. Both featured
quarterlight windows for sightseeing, although 357's
passengers may not have seen much of the Scottish
mountains around Oban, judging by the sky!
Richard Delahoy collection; Alan Osborne

EASTERN NATIONAL
HOLIDAY TOURS

EXCURSION
PROGRAMME
No. 13
Eastern *National*

EXCURSIONS & TOURS

1963

LONDON

From St. OSYTH BEACH & St. Osyth Village (School Square), etc.

ENOC gained managerial control of the Tillings Travel fleet in 1962, although the fleets were kept separate until February 1970. There were frequent swaps of coaches between the two fleets, and the Tilling vehicles were given ENOC-style numbers, with a T prefix, from August 1964. A committed AEC user in the 1950s, Tillings latterly standardised on Bristol/ECW products, as evidenced by this pair of Bristol MW coaches, T318 (1 BXB) and T330 (BPU 24B). They would later join the ENOC fleet, initially as coaches (numbered 383 and 310 respectively), but both would be rebuilt by Marshall in 1974/5 with power doors, roof-mounted destination screens and bus seats as 1440 and 1450 respectively, surviving in that form until 1978 (1450) and 1980 (1440). *Photobus*

A fascinating shot showing newly delivered Tillings Transport Bristol RELH/ECW coach T400 (AOO 18B) in Tilling red and cream at ENOC's Central Works in 1964. It would not join the ENOC fleet until 1970, however, initially as 422 but renumbered 1613 in 1975, although it had been relegated to dual-purpose duties in 1971. *Photobus*

More unusual coach deliveries in 1968 comprised a quartet of the short RESH chassis with Duple Commander bodies, like 413 (YTW 537F), seen here on tour in Yeovil. In 1971 all four moved across into the Tilling fleet, by then renamed as Tillings Travel (NBC) Ltd, before passing to National Travel (South East) in 1974. At some stage this particular coach was fitted with an air-conditioning plant, involving the extension of the rear overhang by about a foot to accommodate the necessary trunking, as illustrated in Duncan Roberts' history of the Bristol RE.
Alan Osborne

Eastern National was a relatively late convert to the RE bus. Having cancelled a 1964 order, it did not take any until 1969, when the first 20 of an eventual fleet of 55 heralded the more widespread introduction of one-man operation. No 1503 (CVW 857G), one of the first batch of five, is seen between the bus station and the ENOC garage in Colchester.
Richard Delahoy collection

▲ The first five Bristol VRs also arrived in 1969, but not all were used immediately as OMO buses; Bill Cansick's shot of 3002 (CPU 981G), taken in Basildon yard 13 months after delivery, shows it still to be a crew bus, double-deck OMO being viewed with suspicion at the time. Indeed, the first buses had to be fitted with automatic passenger-counting devices to allow the driver to monitor the upper-deck load, but the equipment soon fell into disrepair! The first five VRs all arrived in bus livery, but four were repainted immediately into DP colours for the X10; after complaints of rough riding they were soon moved to other duties.
W. T. Cansick / Paul Harrison collection

◄
▼ A foretaste of the 1970s, showing firstly Bristol RELL 1535 (MHK 917J) resplendent in Tilling green/cream, shortly before the NBC livery edicts took effect, on layover in Colchester in the company of 2211 MK, an ex-demonstrator AEC Bridgemaster in the fleet of Osborne's of Tollesbury. The lower picture is of one of the 15 VRs received from Alexander (Midland) in exchange for FLFs. No 3013 (SMS 39H) shows how they ran in 1971, in Alexander blue, finally bringing double-deck OMO to the X10, now renumbered 400 and already in decline. But that, as they say, is a story for another day. *Richard Delahoy; Alan Osborne*

This shot of Bristol L5G ONO 49 at East Hanningfield could have been taken at almost any time since 1950, when the bus was new. In fact, it represents the preservation era and was taken in 1989, hence the red 'PG' depot plate, denoting 'Preservation Group' — not an official ENOC code! Inset we see the same vehicle, after sale by ENOC in 1964 (to a dealer, who passed it on to Bolton-based contractor Seddon in 1965) and before being saved for preservation by the late Terry Coughlin, then a body fitter at ENOC's Prittlewell works. The author was privileged to help Terry with ONO's first restoration. *Richard Delahoy; Richard Delahoy collection*

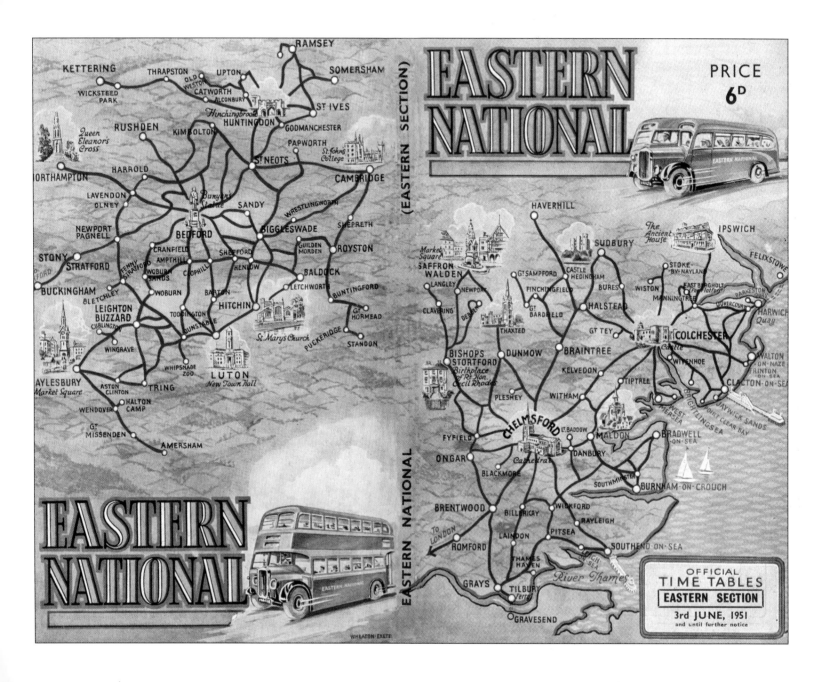